BACK ROAD TO PROGRESS

Documented Accounts of the Historical Civil Rights Movement in the United States and Its Impact on One Family's Decision to Engage in the End to Public School Segregation in Virginia Beach, Virginia

Through the lens of a child: "I was six years old. I didn't understand this thing called integration, but I knew it was important."

Dr. C. Elaine McCoy Smith

ISBN 979-8-88832-671-8 (paperback)
ISBN 979-8-88832-672-5 (digital)

Christian Faith Publishing
832 Park Avenue
Meadville, PA 16335
www.christianfaithpublishing.com

Printed in the United States of America

In memory of my father, George "Ruffin" McCoy; my sister Rubye Renà McCoy; Mr. Junius Gills, a community leader; and to all the other Black children who participated in this effort, all of whom made significant contributions toward the desegregation of public schools in Virginia Beach (formally known as Princess Anne County), Virginia. I give you homage for your sacrifices, support, and input in bringing this book to actualization.

Contents

Preface

To the beloved reader, thank you for giving your valuable time to read the accounts of one child's experience of desegregation in the southeast of America. It is the author's hope that through accounts of some of the historical civil rights events throughout the United States that are depicted here and those that impacted my family, you, too, will gain knowledge and reflect on where you and your family members were during these periods of time. The old school candy Tootsie Roll Pops (colorful on the outside but all chocolate on the inside) was used in a simple analogy by my dad to explain to me (a five – to- six- year- old) regarding racial differences that "we may be different on the outside, but we're exactly the same on the inside."

The intent of the author is to document these accounts to enlighten and stretch your minds so you may have a better understanding of the plight of many African American families who have evolved through decades of unfair treatment and many of the events that have been pivotal to the understanding of why Black Lives Matter in America. Additionally, I pray that you too, regardless of your ethnicity, can share your life's stories so that we, as the human race (the only race that matters), will become more tolerant of each other and realize that we are more similar than different and that we are all God's children and should be striving to leave this world better off because we were in it as we work together toward the ultimate goal of a colorless eternity.

Acknowledgments

I would like to take this opportunity to give thanks to those who have been instrumental in encouraging, inspiring, motivating, and supporting me in the process of bringing this book to fruition.

First, I'd like to thank God for guiding me not just through the process of writing this book but for his grace and mercy that has kept me through the trials and tribulations of my life and the lives of those connected to me. It is my prayer that the contents of this work, which is based on my truth, are pleasing to him and ignite a desire for the reader to engage in courageous conversations to end racism that is perpetuated on so many levels throughout our nation and the world. It is through this type of transparency that we can and will continue the healing process of our community and nation.

My dad was the inspiration for the book. I was too young to fully understand the significance of integration of public schools. However, in his infinite wisdom, he had the ingenious ability to use practical analogies to explain to me the importance of our plight, which gave meaning to the struggle. It was he, along with my mother, who instilled in me the spirit of boldness and assertiveness that gave me a lifelong demeanor of courage in the face of adversity.

My deceased sister Rubye (our family called her by her middle name, Renà) and I entered this journey together. At the time, we were the only two Black children at Kempsville Elementary School in Virginia Beach, Virginia. As we grew older, we often discussed our experiences and were always committed to documenting our story, if no more than just for our family history. Her memory has been a constant presence throughout the entire writing process of this work. We experienced overwhelming bullying, ridicule, and racial tension in the first couple of years. But for me, that first year, with her by my side, gave me comfort. She was a fifth grader and had a better understanding of the goal of our purpose during this endeavor. Her sweet disposition, mild manner, kind heart, and insistence that we ignore the ongoing mental and frequent physical abuse helped me to endure the bullying by pretending that it did not bother me (although it did). She gave me the strength to persevere through most of it without visible scars. I thank God that she was there.

In 2010, when I first toyed with the idea of writing this book (of course, life events seemed to readily divert my attention, and it has taken a lot longer than anticipated), Mr. Junius Gills was the only living member (president) of the civic organization where he, my dad, and two others were the driving force behind the end to desegregation in public schools in Princess Anne County, Virginia. Through a face-to-face interview, he provided firsthand accounts, documented evidence, and gave additional insight into the rationale for the initial movement toward public school desegregation. Mr. Gills passed away at the age of eighty-four the following year (2011), but I thank him and his family for providing information that I did not have, clarifying some of what I thought I knew, and validating facts in which I was sure of.

To my best friend, Donald P. Smith, my husband. Thank you for over thirty years of marriage. The journey that we've shared and your constant support through each endeavor are what have propelled me to a place of self -awareness, reflection, and consciousness to boldly document my truth. Without your support, I'm not sure that this book would have come to life.

You have been a sounding board for my scattered recollections of the past as you encouraged me to research historical events for validity. You get me, and I love and appreciate you for your understanding of my sometimes exhausting efforts for promoting the fair treatment of others and my enthusiasm for working for just causes even when it is not the most popular thing to do.

Thank you to my son, Donovan, and my daughter-in-love, Tia, for keeping it real. Thank you for providing a millennial perspective as to how the relevance of history impacts the thinking of today's youth and acknowledging the importance of knowing your cultural history from shared stories of the past. How can you respect what you don't know? I love the freethinkers that you are and how you study God's Word together, navigating through these chaotic times as you strive to fulfill his purpose for your lives. It is because of you that I was compelled to complete this endeavor so that you have a foundation for a piece of our family's history to share with your own offspring, Gia and Van, the current brightest lights in my life.

Chapter 1

Embryonic Stage of Change

Knock, knock, knock. I listened at my parents' door. "Daddy? Ma-Mè? I don't feel good."

My mother answered in the most nurturing tone, "Yeah. Come in, baby. What's wrong, Elaine?"

I was experiencing dry heaves and an upset stomach in anticipation of what was in store for me on the first day of my second-grade schoolyear. This was the beginning of what is now known as the end to desegregation in Virginia Beach, Virginia, public schools, formally known as Princess Ann County, Virginia.

I started first grade at age five as I had been taught most of what was expected of kindergartners at home by my older siblings. My parents often expressed their delight that people were always commenting to them about how bright I was.

In church Sunday school and plays, I read well for my age and always remembered my lines quickly. I could not only recite my lines with boldness but also knew what everybody else was supposed to say and do as well.

There was an informal community school where Black children in the area communities attended for basic readiness skills. My mother shared that she was told by the woman from our church Mrs. Thomas (fictitious name) who ran the school that I already had those basic skills. When I turned five in February, I was provided the opportunity to attend the second semester of first grade in March with my cousin Jerry, who was two years older than me. There was no formalized pre-kindergarten at that time. His teacher, a friend of the family, noticed that I was more or at least as mature as many of the children in his class and recommended that I be promoted to the first grade the next year instead of going to kindergarten, even though I wouldn't be six until February.

I was anything but shy, and I remember at times being told by my family that I needed to "stay out of grown folk's conversations" and mind my business. I've loved to talk all of my life and have an opinion about everything, warranted or not. Education was important to my parents, George "Ruffin" McCoy and Rosana Holloman McCoy, as we children were told frequently that it was the gateway to our future.

We lived on Whitehurst Landing Road in Princess Ann County. (It was known as the "back road" to the New Light community on Indian River Road, the Black community closest to our home. Thus, the title of this book.)

We were raised as Christians (Baptist) and were members of a small community church called New Light Baptist Church, which was also on Indian River Road in Princess Anne County.

In the early days, it was our entire extended family's home church way before I was born. There were uncles, aunts, cousins, and grandparents—all with the McCoy last name and who were leaders in the church. In our home, we regularly practiced reading the Bible as a family activity, and every Sunday morning before church, we read scripture selected by my dad or mom and discussed its lesson or the lesson from that week's Sunday-school book, recited Bible verses, and prayed before breakfast. I'm smiling as I write, reminiscing the smell of my mother's homemade rolls that were in the oven for dinner to go along with the collard greens and neck bones and rice, fried chicken, and potato salad, which had been prepared for dinner early that morning or the night before (yummy). Though we would have already had breakfast, cornflakes with milk (Carnation or made from a powder or fresh cow's or goats' milk), we would all get a hot buttered roll before piling into the car and heading out to church. I think I focused more on getting that roll than the actual Bible verse for the day.

I remember a white two-story house near our house in rural Princess Ann County, where foster children lived. I thought those children were my friends—that is, until we started going to school together. There was a potato/pea field (depending on the season) where we played when there were no crops planted. It separated the land of the owners from ours. They had a cow, and we sometimes got fresh milk from them.

We had a couple of pigs, a goat, and chickens. And my grandfather Linwood McCoy, who lived just down the lane, farmed every vegetable that you could think of—to name a few, collards, kale, string beans, cucumbers, butter beans, turnip greens, and so on. He also had cherry and peach trees and a small vineyard where the best grapes and blackberries grew, so we often bartered for fresh milk.

Generations of Racial Tension

Labels play a significant role in defining many things, including groups and individuals who belong to the group. This has been especially true for racial and ethnic groups in general and for Blacks in particular. For decades, the standard term for the Black diaspora has shifted from *Colored*, *Negro*, and *Black* to *African American* and now is included when speaking of "people of color." The changes have been viewed as attempts by Blacks to redefine themselves and to gain respect and standing in a society that has held them to be subordinate and inferior in the eyes of the majority of society.

The ethnic terms *Colored, Negro, Black*, and *African American* will be used interchangeably, depending on the decade that is being referred to. Please be mindful as I venture through the accepted schizophrenic rhetoric that my culture has been referred to as in excess of the last sixty years.

For the reader to fully understand the impetus for change that my parents sought after, it is important to realize what was happening throughout the nation to steer them to yearn for equality. Not just for themselves but for the future of their children and their children's children. Presented throughout this book are brief synopses of documented historical events surrounding civil rights that I believe impacted my parents' thinking.

During my parents' lifetime, the early struggles of the Civil Rights Movement were evident throughout Virginia, the nation, and the world. It continues today based on the current issues with racial tensions where the fires have been fanned by the forty-fifth president's (Trump) rhetoric and the apparent inequality that is witnessed on so many fronts for Black and Brown people.

Moving forward, the focus of the contents of this book will remain on what was occurring within the United States with the documentation of historical facts regarding the Civil Rights Movement locally and nationally, aligning them with demographics of my family so that the increasing urgency for change that my parents encountered can be realized by the reader. (The local facts headings will be italicized.)

So that the reader can envision the racial tension and civil rights issues that were apparent during my parents' childhood and young adult life, it is important to review the history of the lack of inclusion (desegregation) that existed during their formative years, which, I predict, must have prompted them to move forward to embrace public school integration when the opportunity presented itself. You will find that many segregation issues impacted the decisions for other changes regarding integration as well.

History

1924

Racial Integrity Act passed. Native Americans are barred from White schools.

My father was born in 1922 and my mother in 1927. Though education was limited, they received what was available (usually a one-room schoolhouse with several grades in one class). My dad, the son of a farmer, spent most of his school days during harvest season (in which there was always some harvest to be gathered) in the fields, as that was his family's vocation. Each item on the subsequent time line was experienced by my parents, and I believe these aided in the decision to engage in the integration initiative when they felt the time was right, for their children.

1936

The Dovell Act is passed. Gives scholarships for Black college students to be educated out of state.

1940

Federal court rules Norfolk School Board violated Fourteenth Amendment by not paying Black and White teachers equally.

Movements for civil rights were a worldwide series of political movements for equality before the law that peaked in the 1960s. In many situations, it took the form of campaigns of civil resistance aimed at achieving change through nonviolent forms of resistance. In some situations, it was accompanied, or followed, by civil unrest and armed rebellion. The process was long and tenuous, and many of these movements did not fully achieve their goals, although the efforts of these movements did lead to some improvements in the legal rights of previously oppressed groups of people.

The main aim of the movements for civil rights included ensuring that the rights of all people were equally protected by the law, including the rights of minorities, women's rights, and lesbian, gay, bisexual, and transsexual (LGBTQ) rights.

Chapter 2

Agents for Change

Daddy

George "Ruffin" McCoy Sr. was the fourth of twelve children. As a child, he knew nothing more than the hard life of a farmer's son and church. He had two siblings who would die early in life, but I am unaware of the cause of their deaths. He was aware of the racial unrest, and his experience with racism was what he experienced, saw, and heard of locally. Even then, he was being told by his parents how to best respond when approached by the White man: "yes sir," no eye contact, humble yourself, no aggression, be careful at night, and the like.

My dad joined the military at age nineteen. He served as a cook in the US Navy during World War II and Korean War. During those days, the United States Navy commands were segregated, and Dad formed relationships with many Negroes from around the nation who were in the same battalion. They were all treated as second-class citizens in the States but were good enough to fight their war. The conversations between the Negro men from various states around the nation enhanced his understanding, and he learned that his comrades were experiencing the same types of civil unrest involving the Ku Klux Klan, or KKK. (The Ku Klux Klan is a secret society in the Southern United States that focused on White supremacy and terrorized other groups with racial mistreatment.)

As a young man, he was familiar with them as they, too, were highly active in Virginia.

During conversations with those from other states about home, he was told of the Red Summer, where, in 1919, White sailors recently home from the war had been on a days-long drunken rampage, assaulting and, in some cases, lynching Black people on the capital's streets. The relentless onslaught proved contagious, escalating in dozens of cities across the US. It was widespread, and in many places, they were initiated by White servicemen and centered upon the 380,000 Black veterans who had just returned from the war. Because of their military service, Black veterans were seen to be a threat to Jim Crow and racial subordination. That event occurred prior to Daddy's birth in 1922, but hearing about it was the beginning of his understanding that the experiences that he had encountered in a small town called Princess Anne County, Virginia, were just a nugget in comparison to what was happening around the nation.

Dad learned of traumatic events as well as some attempts at progressive Negro moves that occurred during his lifetime, such as Black Wall Street, a community of Black people that was self-sustaining through entrepreneurship and business ownership (such as banks, doctors, lawyers, electricians, plumbers, tailors, etc.) and the Rosewood Community in Florida, each of which had been met with defeat due to racial tensions. He began to ponder how that could occur in his own community as he became aware that farming was not the only option for him. He wanted to pursue other opportunities.

After his time in the war, Daddy was honorably discharged. At that time, he had three children under the age of four and one on the way. He knew that he wanted more for his family, which would require him to increase his income. In his civilian life, he worked as a supply truck driver for the naval air station in Norfolk, Virginia. And as he was also a farmer's son, he assisted his dad and brothers in farming the family land. However, he never forgot what he had learned in the navy and often spoke of our community being self-sustaining. He wanted to pursue more education so that he could have his own business to provide a financial safeguard for his family.

He pursued a certification as a licensed plumber from Booker T. Washington (BTW) High School in Norfolk, Virginia. BTW night school was the only affordable adult education school in Tidewater where Negroes could further their education at the time.

After receiving training and certification, Daddy and his friend Mr. Thomas Jones from Centerville Turnpike (another small Negro community in Princess Anne County) formed a business, as did many African American men during that time.

Not many Negro families in our area had indoor plumbing, but the idea of the construction of indoor bathrooms was blossoming, so business was booming. There was also the ongoing need for repairs in other communities, which also kept additional income coming into the house.

Throughout the Black communities, they were known as established plumbers who could get the job done.

Ma-Mè

My mother, Rosana Holloman McCoy, was the youngest girl of fifteen children in her family. She experienced much devastation in her early life. She was witness to and was told of the other family's experiences of suspected arson as their home was set on fire and burned to the ground two times. This led to the passing of two of her older siblings who had been severely burned in the house while attempting to save other family members. I'm told these occurrences always happened in the late night or early morning hours.

My mother never knew her biological father as she was just an infant when he died. I am uncertain if he, too, was a victim of one of those fires. Word of mouth was that the family's property on Bonney Road was valuable to the City/County as Interstate 64 was planned to expand, and though pressured, my grandmother, Mama Carrie, was not willing to sell. It was suspected that the Ku Klux Klan was responsible for the fires. It was sold, however, after she passed away.

Her brother's (Uncle Bud) property—which is now a part of Mount Trashmore, a recreational and tourist site in Virginia Beach, Virginia—was sold to the City. And it was rumored that it was under duress. During those days (I'm told), there was little to no legal investigation for Negroes; therefore, no one was ever questioned or charged, considering who the suspects were. Also, there was no Black representation on the local police force that they could turn to.

I can only imagine the challenge of, year after year, having to start over as most everything was lost in the fires. What is certain is that, throughout the years, crosses were visibly burned on the site adjacent to my great-uncle's property. When he sold, they moved into our old family home on our property, where stories were told of these encounters.

My mother often told us of how her eldest sister—Aunt Vickie, who relocated to the North—would send her clothing from New York so that, as a girl and teen, she would have the latest fashion to wear. (Back then, relocating to the North was common as there were more employment opportunities and less overt racism.)

In February of 1944, Ma-Mè (as we affectionately called my mother) married at age sixteen. She was pregnant and had six children by 1959. I was her fifth child, and Duane (the baby at the time) was the sixth of seven children that she would eventually have.

She had decided that motherhood, though rewarding, did not satisfy her yearning to have other adult interactions. She wanted to earn her own income and to gain employment outside of the home. She had three boys and three girls by this time, and I suspect, with all the discussion regarding women's rights, that she wanted to model a woman's independence for both her girls and boys. She, too, wanted more for herself and our family, and she began researching her interest in home nursing—more specifically, midwife services for pregnant women. So she pursued nursing.

My oldest sister, Vera, a teenager, was left in charge of the rest of us while she, too, went to school at night at BTW High.

One of the fondest childhood memories I have of my mother is seeing her going to school and watching her diligently studying at the kitchen table for her nursing certification. I often overheard her say to my oldest sister, "It's important to have your own money. Women cannot just sit around and wait on men to give them everything that they need and want." She was determined to be a midwife as she figured that she knew quite a lot about birthing babies since she had five babies at home herself. There was limited affordable hospital care during those days.

Norfolk Community Hospital (originally established in 1915 with only thirty beds) was the only hospital where colored/Negroes could receive care. Unable to provide quality care due to financial issues, through grants, it was eventually moved to a site and upgraded to more modern standards. However, with only seventy beds, they were considered a small hospital and were limited to the number of persons who could receive care at the hospital.

Ma-Mè and my daddy worked out a plan after he finished his plumbing certification so that she could continue her education as well. She graduated at the top of her class. I often watched her in admiration as she got dressed, wearing her starched all-white nursing uniform and hat, opaque white stockings, and soft-sole nursing shoes. It was quite different from the colorful smocks and crocks worn by medical staff today. She was employed by many facilities (Holmes Convalescent Home for the Elderly and Lake Taylor Hospital), but her most rewarding positions were when she was later employed at Norfolk General Hospital, currently known as Sentara Norfolk General Hospital.

She worked in the intensive care unit and the emergency room, and she landed her dream spot when she was in the nursery with the babies. She did pursue midwife work on the side for a few years with community moms who continued to have babies at home. I admired her so much that, at one point in my childhood, I thought I wanted to become a nurse just like Ma-Mè until I realized that I really didn't have the fortitude for seeing lots of blood or witnessing the pain of others. This became apparent when my brother Duane (the baby boy) and I were running inside to answer a phone call in anticipation that our oldest brother, George Jr. (Bubba), was returning home from Vietnam. Duane tripped on the step, and his arm went through the glass pane in the door, leaving a gaping gash. Blood rapidly poured from his arm. There was so much blood that I felt faint. So my older sister Ruby Renà and I (we had been left in charge of him as my mom and dad worked) took turns running warm water over his arm, not knowing that we were exasperating the situation.

Remember, there were no cell phones, and we did not dare call my mom at work. When Ma-Mè got home from work several hours later (she worked the seven-to-three shift), my brother was so weak that he leaned on the sink (we had given him a chair from the kitchen to sit at the sink), and he would drift off to sleep from exhaustion as he had been crying a lot.

Though she was clearly upset, she never chastised us for what we had done. She only explained that pressure on the wound with a clean cloth was what was needed to slow the blood flow. It was then that I knew nursing was not for me.

Chapter 3

The Way We Were

We lived on land acquired by my grandfather and passed down to his sons to farm. We initially had a small house with no indoor plumbing. We had an outdoor pump that required priming to get water from a well. (Priming a well pump means you're removing the air from the pump and filling it with water, which is necessary for the pump to work properly.) There was a bucket that hung on the handle of the pump. It was filled with water to pour into the pump to initiate the priming process. We also had an outdoor toilet that I used sparingly due to the lizards and spiders that I had seen scurrying around the outside of the outhouse from time to time.

In the winter, the pump would freeze, and my older brothers were taught by my dad to build a fire around the metal pipes to thaw them so we could get water to cook, bathe, and drink. I shared a bedroom with my older sisters Vera Lee and Rubye Renà. We all slept in one full-size bed, with them on each side at the top and me in the middle at the foot of the bed with Vera's toes always seemingly in my face. I remember tickling her toes frequently as she did mine when we lay in bed.

My parents maximized every foot of the two-bedroom house as my brothers George (Bubba) and Ronald (Ronnie) also shared the same room with the girls. There was a floating wall that divided the room in half. (It was a sheet used as a curtain.) The boys slept in bunk beds on the other side. There were no closets. Our few dress clothes hung from hangers on nails around the walls. Our everyday play/school clothes, socks, and underwear were neatly folded in the drawers of the bureaus (chest of drawers). We had two of them back-to-back, one for the boys and the other for the girls. Everyone liked having his or her own drawers.

Duane, the baby, slept in his crib in my parents' room.

The growing size of our family prompted my parents' discussion regarding the need for a larger home. The obvious need encouraged my dad to build another house on the same property as our family had begun to burst at the seams. Three additional children had joined the family since we had originally moved into the home, two toddlers and a baby. Daddy enlisted support from some of his friends and brothers who had become skilled laborers as well. Uncle Frank was a certified electrician, and I don't recall who the carpenter and brickmason were, but nevertheless, I remember that they all pitched in and worked together to build our house as well as their own.

As kids, we were frequently told not to enter the construction site when my dad was not there, but I remember one time when the Sheetrock had recently been installed. I was four or five when we all climbed up on the ladder and were taking turns walking the two-by-fours, and my foot slipped and went through the ceiling. I will put this mildly. We were lined up (except for my oldest sister, Vera, who was in the other house taking care of the baby, Duane, and preparing dinner) from the oldest brother, Bubba (George Jr.), to me (the youngest), and each was given a good swatting. The oldest received the worst of it because he should have been setting an example for the rest of us and had been told specifically to keep his siblings off the construction site, which literally was next door. I got more of a tongue-lashing, which was just as devastating as I wanted to do nothing but please my dad, and he was not happy.

During that time, we had one black-and-white TV (which eventually had a wire clothes hanger hanging out of the back as an antenna and a pair of pliers to turn the channel selector for the five channels available at that time), one black rotary phone (I still recall the number: KI5-2204), and one car that resembled the PT Cruiser from the early 2000s.

In our area, in what was then known as Princess Ann County, city transportation only ran on Saturdays, with one pickup in the New Light community and one stop on Granby Street in downtown Norfolk, Virginia. There were not many stores that colored/Negroes could patronize, so frequenting department stores was not something that we did as a family. Usually, Mom would allow us to look at the JCPenney and Sears catalogs, and my sister and I would choose items that we liked by marking them or folding the pages of the catalogs. Our clothes were purchased by our parents, and we had no say in the choices made. It was what you had, and it was what you wore.

When I was old enough (I'll say around eleven), my older sister Renà and I, after all the chores were done on Friday night, were given permission to walk the path through the woods to the New Light community to catch the bus on some Saturday mornings in the summer to go to downtown Norfolk.

We purchased school clothes with the money we had earned working in the fields, picking cucumbers. (I will get back to my distaste for "picking" cucumbers later.) We had become accustomed to the stares, grunts, and comments from people who did not look like us, and we understood the urgency of being at the bus stop on time as there was only one bus run in the morning and one in the evening. We were cautioned by our parents not to miss the evening bus and get stranded in Norfolk with no way of getting back home to Virginia Beach as the one family car was usually being used on Saturdays for my dad's plumbing business.

The McCoys were an esteemed family in our community, though to today's standards, we were poor. I didn't know that though, as I was never hungry and always got whatever I knew to ask for. My grandfather Linwood McCoy ("Dad-Lin" and his sons) shared from our harvest as we lived off the land, and it was nothing to exchange eggs from the chicken coop and cucumbers, collards, butter beans, string beans, kale, and turnip greens from the fields and ham and sausage from the hogs and so on in return for milk from cows and goats or other resources and services that neighbors may have had to barter with. No matter what the season, there was always plenty to eat and a harvest to gather, freeze, and store for the future.

There was one community grocery store, Acredale Grocery Market, and my great-aunt Beulah ran a small convenience store (she's the first Black female entrepreneur that I am aware of in our family) next to the church. And another small store—owned by Ms. Tabb, the candy lady—was farther down the street on the opposite side of the church. My uncle Johnny McCoy was the original male entrepreneur in the family, as well as an agriculturist who sold fruits and vegetables from his truck in the marketplace in downtown Norfolk.

Color-Blind

Color was unimportant to me before I started school. Don't get my words twisted as I could see the visual difference and knew that there were Black and White people, but I never knew it was an issue. It was just the way it was. I was from a family of many hues. My mother was of a dark complexion and my dad of a light complexion, and their children were every color in between. My brother Ronnie, as we got older, would tell community guys that he had four sisters and would ask, "What color do you want?"

I smile as I'm writing this as he was the comedian of the family and always had us laughing. We were just children who enjoyed running, racing, laughing, and climbing trees. I climbed trees faster and higher than any of the boys.

Virginia Beach was quite rural in those days with no next-door neighbors in the sense of today's standards. Our neighbors were the Smiths. Mr. Booker T. and Ms. "Shug" had a son around my age—Arnold, my archrival who lived down the lane. Our houses were separated by about two acres of fields. They were also part-time farmers. As children before integration began, all we knew was to do our chores and play with the White foster kids who lived close to us in an old white two-story house on Whitehurst Landing Road across from the pea/potato or soybean field, depending on the season. Later, that land was developed, and it is now known as the Homestead Community, initially an "all-White community."

The Journey to McCoy

George "Ruffin" McCoy and Rosana Holloman McCoy
Married February 23, 1944

My parents were married for twenty-seven years before the passing of my dad in 1971, at which time they had seven children.

My elder siblings—Vera (born August 1944), George ("Bubba," born August 1945), and Ronald ("Ronnie," born November 1947)—were all born prior to the executive order signed by President Harry S. Truman, which called for equality of treatment and opportunity for all people. However, it had not been enforced in Virginia.

They attended Princess Anne County Training School, the only school that Negro children could attend. In the early days, it was graded first to twelfth grades, and later, it became the only high school for Negroes in Princess Ann County as Virginia Beach was known during those days. Its name changed to Union Kempsville High School later so that it could be recognized as a high school and not simply a training school to assist in alleviating college admission issues.

Princess Anne County Training School / Union Kempsville High School

Princess Anne County Training School was the first high school for African Americans in Princess Anne County (now known as Virginia Beach). The school was a result of the African American community in the 1930s working together to raise money to build a school so their children could receive a proper education.

The initial money raised was used to purchase four acres of land on Witchduck Road. The land and $2,000 were given to the school board, but no attempt to build a school was made. So in 1934, a temporary school was established on the property of the Union Baptist Church. In 1938, a four-room high school was finally built. Between 1949 and 1962, several additions were made to the school.

The onset of the Civil Rights Movement in the early 1960s impelled the Black citizenry of Princess Anne to think differently about the Black high school in the county being called a training school. The school board voted to rename Princess Anne County Training School as Union Kempsville High School, effective at the start of the 1961–1962 school term.

In 1962, the two-square-mile (5.2 km²) resort town of Virginia Beach became an independent city, followed by the rest of Princess Anne County with whom it was reunited and politically consolidated by mutual approval of residents to form a new independent city in 1963. The Princess Anne County Training School also changed its name to Union Kempsville High School. And in 1969, Union Kempsville High School graduated its last class due to the citywide integration of schools.

By 1965, a federal mandate for school desegregation initiated "freedom of choice" in Virginia Beach. Segregated schools were eventually eliminated in the city, and the Black high school had to permanently close its doors.

Today, the legacy of the school continues with the establishment of the museum, which shares stories of family, community, sacrifice, and the importance of education.

1947

In a precursor to the *Brown* case, a federal appeals court strikes down segregated schooling for Mexican American and White students (*Westminster School Dist. v. Mendez*). The verdict prompts California governor Earl Warren to repeal a state law calling for the segregation of Native American and Asian American students.

1948

President Truman orders the desegregation of the Armed Forces. Chesterfield, King George, and Gloucester Counties ordered to equalize Black and White schools.

July. Truman signs Executive Order 9981, which states, "It is hereby declared to be the policy of the president that there shall be equality of treatment and opportunity for all persons in the armed services without regard to race, color, religion, or nationality.

Arkansas desegregates its state university.

The Supreme Court orders the admission of a Black student to the University of Oklahoma School of Law, a White school, because there is no law school for Blacks (*Sipuel v. Board of Regents of the University of Oklahoma*).

1950

Gregory Swanson enrolls in UVA Law School. He was the first African American student at a White school in Virginia. Black students were admitted to Virginia Tech and the College of William & Mary for programs not available at Virginia State College in the next five years.

Virginia leads the way to *Brown v. Board of Education*. The Supreme Court rules that learning in law school "cannot be effective in isolation from the individuals and institutions with which the law interacts." The decision stops short of overturning Plessy.

The Supreme Court holds that the policy of isolating a Black student from his peers within a White law school is unconstitutional (*McLaurin v. Oklahoma State Regents for Higher Education*).

Barbara Johns, a sixteen-year-old junior at Robert R. Moton High School in Farmville, Virginia, organizes and leads 450 students in an anti-school-segregation strike.

August 30. Rubye (Renà), the fourth child, was born in August 1950. She was given her first name, we were told, because her skin was a very red tone when she was born. She also attended Union Kempsville as an elementary student with her three older siblings.

As she grew older, her fair skin complexion would prove to aid her during the desegregation movement as fair-complexioned Negroes were often treated more fairly than their darker-skinned counterparts. Renà was four years old when the Supreme Court ruled on the landmark case *Brown v. Board of Education of Topeka, Kansas,* unanimously agreeing that segregation in public schools is unconstitutional. And thus the seed was planted in my parents' minds as the beginning glimmer of hope for the future. It would be seven more years before the desegregation ended in Princess Ann County, Virginia.

1951

Students in Farmville protest unequal conditions, then sue for an integrated school. The lawsuit becomes part of Brown v. Board of Education.

1952

The Supreme Court hears oral arguments in Brown v. Board of Education. Thurgood Marshall, who will later become the first African American justice on the Supreme Court, is the lead counsel for the Black school children.

1953

Earl Warren is appointed chief justice of the Supreme Court. A Republican and considered one of the most influential Americans of the twentieth century, his court decisions such as *Brown v. Board of Education, Miranda,* and *Baker v. Carr* have given us such famous phrases as "separate but not equal," "read him his rights," and "one man, one vote" and have vastly expanded civil rights and personal liberties.

1954

The Supreme Court took a momentous step. In a unanimous opinion, *Brown v. Board of Education of Topeka, Kansas,* the court set aside a Kansas statute permitting cities of more than fifteen thousand to maintain separate schools for Blacks and Whites and ruled instead that all segregation in public schools is "inherently unequal" and that all Blacks barred from attending public schools with White pupils are denied equal protection of the law as guaranteed by the Fourteenth Amendment. The doctrine was extended to State-supported colleges and universities in 1956.

1954

May 17. The Supreme Court rules on the landmark case Brown v. Board of Education of Topeka, Kansas, unanimously agreeing that segregation in public schools is unconstitutional. The ruling paves the way for large-scale desegregation. The decision overturns the 1896 *Plessy v. Ferguson* ruling that sanctioned "separate but equal" segregation of the races, ruling that "separate educational facilities are inherently unequal." It is a victory for NAACP attorney Thurgood

Marshall, who will later return to the Supreme Court as the nation's first Black justice.

Brown v. Board of Education

One of the most important legal decisions in US history, the 1954 Supreme Court case Brown v. Board of Education of Topeka, Kansas, declared school segregation unconstitutional and paved the way for the civil rights achievements of the 1960s.

By overturning the "separate but equal" doctrine established in Plessy v. Ferguson (1896), Brown v. Board of Education began the process of unraveling more than half a century of federally sanctioned discrimination against African Americans. As a result, it also initiated a struggle between a government now obligated to integrate all public schools and recalcitrant communities determined to maintain the status quo. This photograph shows an anti-integration rally in Little Rock, Arkansas, on August 20, 1959. The protesters carry American flags alongside placards declaring racial mixing to be "communism" and "the mark of the antichrist"—a fascinating and disturbing mix of patriotism, prejudice, and fear.

At the time of the 1954 decision, laws in seventeen Southern and border states (Delaware, Maryland, Virginia, West Virginia, Georgia, North Carolina, South Carolina, Florida, Tennessee, Kentucky, Alabama, Mississippi, Louisiana, Arkansas, Texas, Oklahoma, and Missouri) and the District of Columbia required that elementary schools be segregated. Four other states—Arizona, Kansas, New Mexico, and Wyoming—had laws permitting segregated schools. But Wyoming had never exercised the option, and the problem was not important in the other three.

Although discrimination existed in the other states of the Union, it was not sanctioned by law.

1955

The court implemented its 1954 opinion by declaring that the federal district courts would have jurisdiction over lawsuits to enforce the desegregation decision and asked that desegregation proceed "with all deliberate speed."

In Brown II, the Supreme Court orders the lower federal courts to require desegregation "with all deliberate speed."

Between 1955 and 1960, federal judges will hold more than two hundred school desegregation hearings.

Chapter 4

A Change's Gonna Come

Hope for the Future

So, you may ask yourself, how was it that this vital information was shared from community to community and state to state? I'm glad you asked. You see, we thought that our parents simply loved to socialize, or so it seemed. On the weekends, we often had company, or we visited other families' and friends' homes.

It was always the latest R & B music and plenty of good food. I now realize that these social events were conducted with purposeful intent. It was a way to disseminate information about the Civil Rights Movement without raising eyebrows outside our community through written communications or phone contact since most Black families had party lines as we did or no phone at all. (A party line is a local loop telephone circuit that is shared by multiple telephone service subscribers. Party line systems were widely used to provide telephone service and were a less expensive option than a private line.)

Face-to-face and word-of-mouth encounters were the preferred or perhaps the safest method of communication at that time. There was always an ongoing campaign for membership recruitment in the National Association for the Advancement of Colored People (NAACP), where much of the nationwide civil unrest was shared with the membership in order that they spread the word with community residents. Thus began our parents' membership in the local chapter of the NAACP along with their children in the youth division.

The NAACP (the National Association for the Advancement of Colored People) is a civil rights organization founded in 1909 to fight prejudice, lynching, and Jim Crow segregation and to work for the betterment of "people of color."

The Doll Test That Began the Discussion

Courtesy of the Library of Congress

Professor and social psychologist Kenneth Bancroft Clark devised a simple test that proved to be a powerful weapon in the NAACP's struggle to end segregation in public schools. In Clark's famous "doll test," Black children between three and seven years old were shown four dolls—two black and two white—and asked to first identify their race.

The children were then asked to express a preference for the dolls by deciding which were "prettier," "better," or which ones they "liked best." The results showed that most Black children preferred the white dolls and, at times, even rejected the black dolls in tears, suggesting that racial prejudice and self-hatred were learned at an early age.

Clark repeated his test in Clarendon County, South Carolina (one of the school districts addressed in Brown v. Board of Education), and served as an expert witness in the South Carolina, Delaware, and Virginia cases that were consolidated into *Brown*. The psychological and social scientific evidence he presented helped convince the court that segregation damaged the social and mental development of Black children.

Again, during those days, there were no cell phones or the internet—just extremely limited visual and printed media reporting for Black people. This news, as did other pertinent information germane to the Negro, traveled locally by means of the local Negro publication the *Journal and Guide*. It was and still is the only newspaper based in Norfolk, Virginia, serving the Hampton Roads area that focused on limited local and national Negro news, sports, and issues. It has been in circulation since the early 1900s.

1955

August. Fourteen-year-old Chicagoan Emmett Till is visiting family in Mississippi when he is kidnapped, brutally beaten, shot, lynched, and dumped in the Tallahatchie River for allegedly whistling at a White woman. Two White men, J. W. Milam and Roy Bryant, are arrested for the murder and acquitted by an all-White jury. They later boast about committing the murder in a *Look* magazine interview. The case becomes a cause célèbre of the Civil Rights Movement.

In 2018, this case was reopened by the United States Justice Department based on the discovery of new evidence. The outcome did not produce any federal charges for a second time, even with the testimony of the White woman who recanted her original accusations. The case was closed in December 2021.

SOURCE: LIBRARY OF CONGRESS

December 1. (Montgomery, Alabama) NAACP member Rosa Parks refuses to give up her seat at the front of the "colored section" of a bus to a White passenger, defying a Southern custom of the time. In response to her arrest, the Montgomery Black community launches a bus boycott, which will last for more than a year until the buses are desegregated on December 21, 1956. As the newly elected president of the Montgomery Improvement Association (MIA), Reverend Martin Luther King Jr. is instrumental in leading the boycott.

1956

Autherine Juanita Lucy is an American activist who was the first African American student to attend the University of Alabama in 1956. Her expulsion from the institution later that year led to the university's president Oliver Carmichael's resignation.

Southern States Try to Destroy NAACP

By the start of 1956, some significant blows had been struck against segregation—among them the *Brown* decision, the ongoing Montgomery bus boycott, and Autherine Lucy's temporary admission to the University of Alabama.

An estimated 49 percent of Americans—61 percent of Northerners and 15 percent of Southerners—believe that Whites and Blacks should attend the same schools.

Tennessee governor Frank Clement calls in the National Guard after White mobs attempt to block the desegregation of a high school.

The Virginia legislature calls for "massive resistance" to school desegregation and pledges to close schools under desegregation orders.

Ma-Mè and Me (Carroll "Elaine" McCoy)

I was born during these historical events. As young parents, having lived through racial inequality themselves, I can only speculate on my parents' desire and the anxiousness simultaneous with the anticipation and hope for the future, for their children to have opportunities not afforded them. By this time, the racial tension across the nation had risen to a critical state. I was named Carroll (spelled with two *r*'s and two *l*'s) purposely (as told to me by my mother) so my gender could not be determined just from the sheer sight of my name on paper.

She said, "I felt like you, at least, would have a fighting chance when employers viewed your application if you were mistakenly confused for a man. You could at least get an interview that you might not have gotten otherwise."

Historically, women were not provided the same opportunities as men then, and sadly, though it is better now, still are not. She had the foresight to attempt to preserve my future and do what she could to give me a fighting chance, at least to get my foot in the door of opportunities. She explained that "Carroll," during those times, was the male spelling or the spelling of one's last name—like Diane Carroll, the only Black female personality on TV that looked like me growing up.

Sometime later, she showed me a picture of this lady in the *Ebony* magazine and reminded me, "That's who you were named after."

She went on to share how, when she applied for my birth certificate, she had to return it twice (paying each time) because they incorrectly spelled my name from *Carroll* to *Carol* or *Carole*. And finally, it came back with *Caroll*, which was still incorrect. I have spelled my first name with two *r*'s and two *l*'s all my life. My high school diploma, bachelor's degree, two master's and doctorate degrees, and my marriage license all display my name spelled that way. Not until well into my adult life, while reviewing my birth certificate, did I realize the error.

1955–56

Dr. Martin Luther King Jr. led Blacks in Montgomery, Alabama, in a boycott against the municipal bus system after Rosa Parks, a Black woman, refused to give up her seat to a White man and move to the segregated section of a bus. The boycott was brought to a successful conclusion when, on November 13, 1956, the Supreme Court nullified the laws of Alabama and the ordinances of Montgomery that required segregation on buses.

1957

The struggle over desegregation now centered upon the school issue. By the end of 1957, nine of seventeen states and the District of Columbia had begun integration of their school systems. The early civil rights dilatory tactics were at least partially successful. After desegregation's first decade, only 2.3 percent of African American children in the Deep South attended integrated schools. But such tactics also tried the patience of African Americans and the federal courts.

Enactment of the 1964 Civil Rights Act in response to the nonviolent Civil Rights Movement finally spurred action. In 1966, the Fifth Circuit Court, in *United States v. Jefferson County Board of Education*, ordered school districts not only to end segregation but to "undo the harm" segregation had caused by racially balancing their schools under federal guidelines.

Jefferson was followed by the Supreme Court's *Green v. County School Board of New Kent County* decision in 1968, requiring desegregation plans that promised to work right away.

January–February. Martin Luther King Jr., Charles K. Steele, and Fred L. Shuttlesworth establish the Southern

Christian Leadership Conference (SCLC), of which King is made the first president.

The SCLC becomes a major force in organizing the Civil Rights Movement and bases its principles on nonviolence and civil disobedience.

According to King, it is essential that the Civil Rights Movement does not sink to the level of the racists and hate-mongers who oppose them. "We must forever conduct our struggle on the high plane of dignity and discipline," he urges.

September. (Little Rock, Arkansas) Formerly all-White Central High School learns that integration is easier said than done. Nine Black students are blocked from entering the school on the orders of Governor Orval Faubus. President Eisenhower sends federal troops and the National  Guard to intervene on behalf of the students, who become known as the "Little Rock Nine."

It is no accident that the pivotal Supreme Court decision launching the modern Civil Rights Movement was an education case, the 1954 *Brown v. Board of Education of Topeka* ruling.

In many ways, the drive to end segregated education and to put African American and White children in the same classrooms was the most radical and potentially far-reaching aspect of the Civil Rights Movement.

Such change was meant to alter the attitudes and socialization of children, beginning at the youngest ages, as well as end the inequality inherent in all "separate but equal" facilities, whether they were drinking fountains, public accommodations, or schools.

The African American struggle for desegregation, according to Gary Orfield, cofounder and director at the Harvard Civil Rights Project and among the nation's leading experts on desegregation, "did not arise because anyone believed that there was something magical about sitting next to Whites in a classroom. It was, however, based on a belief that the dominant group would keep control of the most successful schools and that the only way to get the full range of opportunities for a minority child was to get access to those schools."

The struggle for integrated schools went through several phases since the 1954 decision and has been shaped—both encouraged and constrained—by various court rulings and emotional political and public policy battles. Following *Brown v. Board of Education* (also referred to as *Brown II*, which called for desegregation with "all deliberate speed" in 1955), education became the focus of what was called the South's "massive resistance" to the Supreme Court's rulings.

Massive Resistance

Symbolized most dramatically by Arkansas governor Orval Faubus's order that his state's National Guard unit block the admission of nine African American students to Little Rock's Central High School in 1957. The nearly month-long confrontation ended when President Eisenhower sent in US troops to protect the students. Faubus's action was just one of a variety of methods employed by states and localities to resist implementing the Supreme Court's rulings.

In one prominent example, Prince Edward County, Virginia, abandoned its entire public school system, leaving education to private interests that excluded African American children from their schools. Many African American children were essentially locked out of school for several years until the Supreme Court ruled Virginia's action unconstitutional.

This decision hit close to home for my parents because, at the time, the Negro community in Princess Anne County was still battling with the school board, simply trying to get adequate busing for the only school available where Black children could be educated. This decision spurred them to hope for what they felt was inevitable. Why couldn't their children be educated in the same schools as the White children? I can hear my dad saying, "If it's good enough for them, it's good enough for mine!"

1958

The Supreme Court rules that fear of social unrest or violence, whether real or constructed by those wishing to oppose integration, does not excuse state governments from complying with *Brown* (*Cooper v. Aaron*).

Ten thousand young people march in Washington, DC, in support of integration.

The Norfolk 17

Upper row: Andrew Heidelberg, Louis Cousins, Patricia Godbolt, Carol Wellington, Reginald Young, Alveraze Frederick Gonsouland, Edward Jordan, and Olivia Driver.

Lower row: Betty Jean Reed, Johnnie Rouse, Delores Johnson, *La Vera Forbes*, James Turner Jr., Lolita Portis, Patricia Turner, Claudia Wellington, and Geraldine Talley.

Attorneys who assisted in Norfolk: Victor J Ashe,
J. Hugo Madison, and Joseph A. Jordan Jr.
Resolution of the School Board of the City of Norfolk, Virginia
September 17, 1958

Virginia closed nine schools in four counties rather than have them integrated, but Virginia and federal courts eventually ruled these moves illegal.

1959

Twenty-five thousand young people march in Washington, DC, in support of integration.

Prince Edward County, Virginia, officials close their public schools rather than integrate them. White students attend private academies. Black students do not head back to class until 1963 when the Ford Foundation funds private Black schools. The Supreme Court orders the county to reopen its schools on a desegregated basis in 1964.

1960

Desegregation began in Louisiana. Whites boycotted the integrated New Orleans public schools at first triumphantly—later with diminishing effectiveness.

In New Orleans, federal marshals shielded Ruby Bridges, Gail St. Etienne, Leona Tate, and Tessie Prevost from angry crowds as they enrolled in all-White schools.

1960

February 1. (Greensboro, North Carolina) Four Black students from North Carolina Agricultural and Technical College begin a sit-in at a segregated Woolworth's lunch counter.

Although they were refused service, they stayed at the counter. The event triggers many similar nonviolent protests throughout the South. Six months later, the original four protesters were served lunch at the same Woolworth's counter.

Student sit-ins would be effective throughout the Deep South in integrating parks, beaches, swimming pools, theaters, libraries, and other public facilities.

April. (Raleigh, North Carolina) The Student Nonviolent Coordinating Committee (SNCC) is founded at Shaw University, providing young Blacks with a place in the Civil Rights Movement. The SNCC later grows into a more radical organization, especially under the leadership of Stokely Carmichael (1966–1967).

Country Girl

Again, Princess Anne County was rural during my childhood, and because there were so many of us children (until my older siblings outgrew the children's games), we often found ourselves (after chores) outside playing games that involved running, jumping, climbing—anything that exerted plenty of energy. We played games such as Mother May I?; hopscotch; red light, green light, 1-2-3; hide-and-seek; tag; dodgeball; kickball; jump rope; jacks; marbles; racing; climbing dirt hills; making mud pies; playing school; and finding buttercup flowers to make chain necklaces. At night, we would catch "lightning bugs" (fireflies) to put in jars. We would also catch Japanese beetles and attach thread around their necks and let them fly around. (How inhumane was that?)

My grandfather Linwood McCoy, a farmer, had lots of land. He grew every vegetable and fruit that the Tidewater (previous name for the Hampton Roads area) climate would allow year-round. All his children and grandchildren (and there were many of us), at some point in their lives, and anyone else's child, worked in the collard green, turnip green, mustard green, kale, green bean, butter bean, or cucumber fields.

As an adult, cucumbers are one of my favorite vegetables, but can I say that I hated them as a child though not really understanding why. Let me explain.

Education was a priority to my parents, so my sister (Renà) and I were only required to work in the fields during the summer. From the age of eight to twelve, every summer, from six thirty to approximately five thirty, we worked the cucumber fields, picking bushels of cucumbers for fifteen, twenty, or fifty cents per bushel, depending on the year. (Imagine that!) This was our summer employment to earn money to buy school clothes that we could pick out ourselves. (Where were the child labor laws then?)

We would awaken at five thirty, eat a bowl of cornflakes, and grab our packed lunches, which consisted of mostly a bologna sandwich, a snack, an apple (or whatever fruit was in the house), and a frozen container of water (or sometimes Kool-Aid). My grandfather and, later, my uncle Leonard, who took over for "Dad Lin" when he became too old to manage the day-to-day operations of farming, would sometimes give each of us a bag of chips and a soda before quitting for the day.

(Uncle Leonard was not only a farmer and, later, a City employee, he was also an entrepreneur. He was a community barber and had a barbershop in his garage, where he sold snacks.)

That was a treat for us as we did not get junk food often. We were not mature enough not to be impressed by the treat or to realize that being paid money per basket the day of was a much better incentive (we usually got paid at the end of the week). Nevertheless, it made us kids happy for a few minutes, forgetting all the manual labor that we had endured all day, and it encouraged us to come back the next day (as if we had a choice).

For me, it was *not* what I wanted to do. It was more about not wanting to stay out in the hot sun in the fields with little to no shade. I received huge blisters on my legs from the morning-dew-infecting mosquito bites previously encountered. Scarring on my legs was always a real concern, and I still have visible scars today.

It was usually too hot to wear long pants, but I did eventually, to avoid creating sores on my legs.

I'm ashamed to admit this, but it got to the point where I faked fainting spells so that I could sit in the truck, under the tractor's wagon, or in the shade while my sweet sister Renà would continue to work hard. And she would always split her earnings right down the middle with me, even though I hadn't done half the work.

By the time I was twelve, I had heard older children discussing getting summer jobs with an organization called STOP (Supporting Transformational Opportunities for People: Youth Program), and I swore that when I was old enough, I, too, would not be returning to the fields. There was an age requirement (fourteen or fifteen) and a parental income stipulation. Renà was old enough to participate in the program and had gotten two applications in case she messed up (or so she thought).

I was always considered more mature than my peers, so I (without parental consent) took one of the considerably basic applications and filled it out with a lot of eraser marks. This prompted me to put my age up to fifteen on the application for consideration for the summer work program too.

At the age of thirteen, I secured a job at the Amphibious Base at Little Creek, in the paint shop. Of course, they thought that I met the age requirement of fifteen years and eight months. (There were no computers to verify my age or my parents' income.) My oldest sister, Vera, worked for the administrative office of the organization and knew those who ran the summer youth program, and they knew that Renà and I were her siblings. My sister Renà (my partner in crime) had arranged transportation with a community father (Mr. Peebles) of friends from school, who was transporting his daughters (LaVern and Debra) to and from the same summer job site. I also got a ride.

My parents were livid when they discovered what I had done. My father even threatened that he would not permit me to take the job on the naval base. I assume because he had been a sailor himself, he did not feel that it was appropriate for me to be around so many grown navy men.

After his assessment of the work environment and visiting the site (he knew the civilian workers and the supervisor there), I don't know the conversation details, but I continued to work there that summer and had a summer job in air-conditioning every year thereafter.

No more field work for me!

1961

A federal district court orders the University of Georgia to admit African American students Hamilton Holmes and Charlayne Hunter. After a riot on campus, the two are suspended. A court later reinstates them because of student disorder. They were later returned under a federal judge's order.

In May, mixed groups of Whites and Blacks, called Freedom Riders, undertook a campaign to force integration in bus terminals and challenge segregation in local interstate travel facilities. The buses were attacked by mobs in Anniston, Alabama, where one bus was destroyed by a firebomb. There were riots in Birmingham and Montgomery when Blacks attempted to use facilities previously reserved for Whites. Federal marshals and the National Guard were called out to restore order and escort the Freedom Riders to Mississippi. Many of them were arrested in Jackson, Mississippi, for infractions of the state's segregation laws, and a long series of court battles began. These protests led to an Interstate Commerce Commission ban on segregation in all interstate transportation facilities in 1961.

Final Decision—B. F. Williams Elementary

Bettie F. Williams Elementary opens for Black students. Williams opened in September 1961 with twenty-six classrooms in Princess Anne County. The school housed pupils in grades one through six and served a large section of the county's population. It was named in honor of Mrs. Bettie Forbes Williams, one of Princess Anne County's most illustrious educators. Portsmouth

Public Schools simultaneously admit fourteen Black students to its White schools.

In 2009, an article in the local newspaper regarding the impact of integration in the city of Virginia Beach, Virginia, was published. The superintendent of Virginia Beach schools at the time, E. E. Brickell, was interviewed. He reflected on how the process went off without a hitch (many would disagree) but argued that even though it happened, the end goal of bringing the races together had much work left to do as some schools continued to be segregated based on the communities (zip codes) it served, even at the present day. Evidence shows that this issue continues to be a fact.

My first-grade class was at Betty F. Williams Elementary on Newtown Road in Princess Ann County, Virginia. It was the first newly constructed all-Black elementary school approximately eight miles from our home on Whitehurst Landing Road. This was the only option for Negro children in our area then, never mind that there were two schools less than one and a half miles from our home: Woodstock Elementary and Kempsville Elementary, which were "all-White" schools.

Looking back, I believe, without evidence, that I was being groomed in the first grade for what was yet to come the following year (integration).

I say that because Mrs. Rosalyn Freeman—who, by the way, was the most beautiful Negro woman (not related to me) that I knew—always dressed nice and smelled so pretty. She wore makeup daily with red lipstick. She was one of only two Black teachers that I was ever assigned. Each immensely impacted me in their own way. (My tenth-grade typing teacher, Mrs. Jean Siler, was the other.)

Both taught me valuable lessons that impacted me significantly even into adulthood. Lessons such as to speak in complete sentences, give eye contact when you speak, stand up straight (never cower), have pride in your appearance and your work, lead with confidence, and that there is nothing that girls can't do (preaching "girl power" before this was a popular phrase).

We were in a brand-new school that sparked political interest. Mrs. Freeman would always put me out in front when visitors from the county and state would come to our school to evaluate its effectiveness. These were White administrators who were documenting the efforts of the first Black elementary school in the county. When there were messages or documents that needed to go to the office or to other teachers, she would send me with a note but gave me a verbal message to give as well. I believe it was to assist in the development of my confidence and verbal skills and so on.

Mrs. Freeman was a friend of the family. I believe she and my mother were from the same community in Princess Anne County and went to school together. Mrs. Siler was a stickler for appearance, time management, and work ethic. Whether their favoritism toward me was intentional or not, I credit them both with positively impacting the woman that I am today.

The Wheels on the Bus Go Round and Round

The wheels were about the only thing that worked consistently on the school buses during that time. School bus transportation was a huge issue for the Black community in Princess Anne County as old buses were passed on to the Black schools when the White schools received new ones. They often broke down during school hours to and from school.

During the bitterly cold winter of 1961, Princess Ann County public school transportation to the all-Black schools (Union Kempsville Training School and Betty F. Williams) continued to be inadequate. There was often no heat on the old buses. (There was no air-conditioning either other than some of the half-cracked windows that could not be closed or opened completely in the winter, spring, or summer.) And the buses broke down regularly. There were numerous individual complaints and requests for the safe transporting of Negro children to their designated schools to no avail. Children were often late to and from school due to old and poorly maintained buses from the county. Newly acquired buses were used for the transporting of White students. Again, there were no cell phones, and many homes had only one phone or no phone, so when we were not home at the usual hour, my mother (as did other Negro mothers) had to wait for the fathers to return home from work with the one car (if they had one) to follow the bus route to find out where we were stranded and pick us up.

I remember overhearing a conversation during that bitter winter (I always had my nosy ears open) between my parents regarding a poorly equipped bus with no heat and someone (a female student) who was taken to the doctor's due to numerous days on an unheated bus and allegedly getting a cold that led to pneumonia.

"I am sick of sitting back doing nothing. They pretend to listen to what you have to say and seem to genuinely sympathize with our plight, then they do absolutely nothing, and I am sick of this!" I heard my dad exclaim. This was unusual as I rarely heard him raise his voice.

My mother responded, "Ruffin, I think we all need to come together with one voice. Trying to handle it all individually has less importance. There is power in numbers."

This one conversation in our home fueled the motivation to organize the affected Black communities to band together for the same cause. My dad, George Ruffin McCoy, represented the Negro citizens from Whitehurst Landing Road (also known as "back road"). His brother, Igenter McCoy, represented the New Light community. And there was Mr. Alanta Towns from Queen City along with Mr. Junius Gills from Centerville Turnpike. Together, they formed the Parents and Citizens League of Princess Anne County (PCL-PAC). The original goal of this organization was to push for better transportation for Black children. Ultimately, it turned into much more.

Another five states had some integrated schools by 1961. The states mostly fell back on stopgap measures or on pupil-placement laws, which assigned students to schools ostensibly on nonracial grounds. Forced integration led to much violence.

The most notable instance was the defiance of federal orders by Governor Orval Faubus of Arkansas in 1957. He called out the Arkansas National Guard to prevent integration in Little Rock. President Eisenhower responded by sending federal troops to enforce the court order for integration.

1962

In 1962–63, violence erupted in Mississippi, precipitating a crisis in federal-state relations. Against the opposition of Governor Ross R. Barnett, James H. Meredith, a Black who was supported by federal court orders, registered at the University of Mississippi in 1962. A mob gathered and attacked the force of several hundred federal marshals assigned to protect Meredith. Two persons were killed. The next day, federal troops occupied Oxford and restored order. Meredith became the first African American to attend a Mississippi public school with White students in accordance with the 1954 court decision.

Integration begins at Virginia Beach schools, with thirty-seven Black students approved for the transfer to White schools. They attend Woodstock and Kempsville Elementary and Kempsville Junior High.

Chapter 5

All for One and One for All

Parents and Citizens League of Princess
Ann County (PCL/PAC)

Though these citizens were all active members of the National Association for the Advancement of Colored People (NAACP), the PCL/PAC was a separate entity as its main function was to ensure the safe transporting of the area's Black students to and from school.

JOURNAL AND GUIDE   SEPTEMBER 29, 1962

Toward County-Wide Cooperation

It's all for one and one for all for county-wide civic consideration in Princess Anne now. Shown here are some of the citizens from the various communities in the county who—as representatives of their respective civic organizations, act on matters when they become county-wide.

They are (left to right): A. Town of Queen City, coordinator, George McCoy, advisor; Ijeoma McCoy of New Light, vice-president and Junius Gills of Centerville, president.

Mr. Junius Gills was the president. My uncle, Igenter McCoy, was vice president. Mr. Alanta Towns was the coordinator, and my daddy, George "Ruffin" McCoy, was the community advisor. Also holding positions within the civic organization were Rufus Tabron, Martha Gilchrist, Clifton McCoy, and John Ashby.

I remember my dad expressing to my mom his disappointment in his appearance in this photo for the *Journal and Guide* (the only printed local and national news base for Black people in our area at the time). He had been at work all day and was not able to go home to change into his dress suit in time to get back to the newspaper to take this photograph as the other men did. His resolve was to take position in the back.

My dad passed away from lung cancer nine years after this picture at the age of forty-nine, but my mom held on to these articles for fifteen more years until her passing in 1986. They kept desegregation articles along with other important clippings, which include one of Reverend Dr. Martin Luther King Jr.'s death and a memorial advertisement placed by the renowned Hofheimer's, a leading East Coast shoe retailer, published in the Virginian-Pilot in recognition of King's dedication to civil rights. And there was one of John F. Kennedy's death along with local Black community leaders who made important contributions to the civil rights cause.

In 2012, the articles, which were then fifty years old, were yellow and brittle. And after attempting to retrieve the original documents from the local newspapers (*Ledger-Star*, *Virginian-Pilot*, and the African American newspaper the *New Journal and Guide*) where they were originally published, I found that what I had was more legible than what I had been provided by them. Back then, articles were stored on microfiche, and the duplicating quality was very poor. It was my good fortune to be able to scan a lot of the information that they had kept, which prompted me to research more information about the historical event of the desegregation of public schools in Virginia Beach, Virginia (formally known as Princess Anne County).

In my research, I found handwritten documents listing the names of the thirty-eight Negro children who were being considered for the initial integration movement in Princess Anne County and minutes from meetings held to discuss the next steps.

May 4

Over the spring and summer, student volunteers began taking bus trips throughout the South to test out new laws that prohibit segregation in interstate travel facilities, which include bus and railway stations. Several of the groups of "Freedom Riders," as they are called, were attacked by angry mobs along the way.

The program, sponsored by the Congress of Racial Equality (CORE) and the Student Nonviolent Coordinating Committee (SNCC), involves more than one thousand volunteers, Black and White.

During the summer of 1961 leading up to the summer of 1962, there were numerous meetings that we attended at (as I remember) undisclosed locations to discuss the next steps.

The Greater Good

I learned many years later, as the PCL/PAC moved forward, they realized that there was power in numbers, and what started off as simply trying to achieve adequate busing turned out to be much more. The PCL/PAC was not getting the guaranteed responses from the county school board administration that would afford better transportation for the local Negro students at the "Black schools."

The phrase "if you can't beat them, join them" became the theme of what turned out to be the end to desegregation in Princess Ann County. The Supreme Court had already ruled on the landmark 1954 case in Brown vs. Board of Education of Topeka, Kansas, which unanimously agreed that segregation in public schools was unconstitutional.

The ruling paved the way for large-scale public-school initiative for desegregation, and though it was not the original intent, numerous parents in the Black communities of the New Light, Centerville Turnpike, Whitehurst Landing Road, and Queen City communities in Princess Anne County decided that it was time to move forward and pursue integration in the public (White) schools.

Lessons were learned from the "Norfolk 17" successes and failures; therefore, support was sought from the neighboring county.

At the time, in order to request a transfer to a White school, there was a form that had to be filled out for consideration and approved by the State Board of Education. The problem was that the forms had to be secured from the local school board. However, each time the request was made, there were promises made, but the forms never materialized.

That's where the organizers of the Norfolk 17 came into play. PCL/PAC was able to secure forms that had been used by the Norfolk 17, erased names, and substituted the names of those Black children in Princess Anne County. Once done, and to expedite and ensure that the forms were put in the hands of the education authorities and to alleviate any notion that the request had not been received and date stamped, they were driven directly to the Virginia State Board of Education (one and a half hours away today) for consideration.

It took several hours back then to travel to the state capital, Richmond, Virginia. This was a feat within itself due to the financial constraints (usually, there were only one-car households, no internet to send electronically, and limited interstate highways). The question was whose car could make the trip and who of the PCL/PAC could afford to take off from work as some had jobs where, if you didn't work, you didn't get paid. And they all had families. The group did not dare to travel without reinforcements, so all five men took the journey.

Train Up a Child

We were coached (for lack of a better description) for our roles as agents of social change. The decision to focus on elementary-aged students for the most part was a deliberate intent, as it was said in many of these meetings that it appeared that, nationwide, the older the Negro students were, the more likely that they would be met with violence when supporting the cause. Because nothing could be left to chance, we received age-appropriate instruction in deportment, in managing racial conflict, and in meeting academic challenges. "If they do that, you do this."

As a child, I was always mature for my age, strong-willed, and smart (so I'm told). A teacher from the community (I'll call her Ms. Cross) suggested to my mother that I should be in school. (There was no preschool during those days.) I begged my mother to let me go to school like my older sibling Renà but was told that I was too young. I had a cousin who was in first grade and was two years older than me (Jerry), and in March, after my fifth birthday in February, I went to school with him. His teacher was the same person who had suggested to my mom that I needed to be in school.

At the end of that school year (four months later), because of my achievement, it was recommended that I skip my kindergarten year since it was not mandatory. I was sent on to the first grade at Betty F. Williams that fall. Mrs. Rosalyn Freeman (handpicked by hook or by crook by my mother) was my teacher. I have to say, even as an adult, this was my favorite teacher for many reasons. First, she was always well-dressed and smelled really pretty. Second, although I'm sure she did not consciously feel that I was her favorite, she made me feel as if I were. Lastly, she must have known what the next year would bring, and she would often put me in leadership roles as if she was determined to support my parents' efforts to build inner strength and self-confidence in me. I was always put out in front that year in classroom activities and school plays.

That year (1961) was the first year Bettie F. Williams Elementary, the brand-new elementary school for Blacks, was established. We were taught to take pride in our new environment, and our fall and spring school play's theme centered around school pride. Each class or grade level was to perform. I remembered everyone's part in the play and was used as an assistant to remind other students if they forgot their part. I'm smiling as I write this as it is one of the fondest memories I have of my formative years of school.

As we got closer to the new school year in 1962, my nervous stomach condition became more severe as we continued to attend these meetings now more frequently, and it was clear that Renà and I were expected to be (what we thought) the first Blacks to integrate Princess Ann County public schools. I don't remember other children being at the meetings or who the other adults were, but I do remember the anxious feelings of anticipation whenever the subject of school entered the adult conversation.

Interview with Mr. Junius Gills

My sister Renà and I always discussed documenting our experience during the initial stages of the desegregation of public schools in Princess Anne County, Virginia. But in 2014, she lost her fight with amyotrophic lateral sclerosis (ALS), as did my eldest sister in 2012 of the same ugly disease.

I felt an urgency and was more committed than ever to document our experience. I had bits and pieces of things that I had heard my parents and other adults discussing. I had my own firsthand knowledge of what occurred through my eyes, but my significant clarity was not until my interview in 2010 with the then eighty -three -year -old man Mr. Junius Gills, the only living member who had been the president of the civic organization Parents and Citizens League of Princess Anne County (PCL/PAC).

After explaining my intent, his family was gracious enough to allow me an audience with Mr. Gills. First, he looked just like the picture in the paper from 1962 (just more distinguished). His clarity and attention to detail were phenomenal.

He and I talked and laughed for almost an hour. Mr. Gills and I were able to converse regarding the intimate details of the time that led up to the actual integration event in 1962. I had numerous "aha" moments, and the historical efforts of this organization became clearer to me. Not only did he answer my questions, he confirmed the consensus of the local Negro community during that time, which was "The time for action is *now*." He talked a lot about how it was an ongoing struggle. Mr. Gills, my dad, my uncle, and another gentleman organized to achieve various community support to initially push for better transportation to the Black schools, but their efforts turned out to be so much more. It was amazing as none of these leaders were highly educated but had the wherewithal to accomplish this historical event. When obstacles arose, there would be someone from the group or they knew someone who was able to get the information required to get around the roadblock.

The next pieces of information are documented from the interview and are his accounts of how the local process began. They proceeded despite the obstacles and ended in what he phrased as "a victory for Negroes in Princess Anne County, Virginia."

The historical Norfolk 17 had already struggled with years of pushback but had finally, in February of 1959, claimed victory in integration. A lot of important information gathered during this time was shared with the Parents and Citizens League of Princess Anne County (PCL/PAC) to assist them in facing and combating some of the same issues that Norfolk had encountered. He discussed the local NAACP gaining momentum with the rising membership numbers but that there was a need to establish an organization independent of them for political reasons.

All members of the PCL were members of the local and national NAACP and were overtly and/or covertly, as were local attorneys who had gone to school with Thurgood Marshall. Remember, there were very few higher education institutions that accepted Negroes, so law students usually went to the same schools throughout the nation and developed a brotherhood.

They even legally advised each other so that issues confronting the Civil Rights Movement throughout the nation and lessons learned were realized and not repeated.

While in Mr. Gills's home (the same home that he and his family lived in so many years ago in 1962), he took pride in showing me a bullet hole in the window in his living room, where White teenage "night riders" (his words, not mine) shot into his home. Fortunately, they missed him and his family.

He discussed reporting the incident to the authorities and believed that perhaps one of the kids may have been the child or a relative of one of the local White police officers. According to him and documented by the brittle news clippings I reviewed that were kept by my parents, the Black communities met to discuss the results of the investigation of the shooting as it was not the first incident, and it was decided to protest the lack of follow-through by the police and local authorities. Due to the protest, the three students (ages sixteen and seventeen) were eventually apprehended, and in May 1963, they were placed on probation for what was characterized as "pranks."

Though emboldened, Mr. Gills was still a bit disheartened and felt that their efforts were met with defeat due to the teenager's affiliation with some of the Whites who were involved with the investigation. However, it showed that these communities would stand together and would no longer suffer in silence. This was the power of the community coming together, speaking and being heard with one voice, even though this time little was done. It was bittersweet.

1962

The end to segregation.

In the fall of 1962, thirty-eight Negro students integrated schools in Princess Ann County at Woodstock Elementary, Kempsville Elementary, and Kempsville Junior High.

There were several students who entered Woodstock Elementary and Kempsville Junior High who had the camaraderie of each other, but my sister Renà and I were the only two Negro students at Kempsville Elementary that first year. With the exception of the janitor, maid, and cafeteria workers, no one else in the entire school looked like us. I was in the second grade and Renà was in the fifth. We were old enough to have some understanding of what our efforts meant for ourselves and for others who would follow. Everything that had occurred that was captured through the media throughout the nation regarding the move for integration was shared at home and in our "secret" meetings so that we were well prepared for what we possibly could and, in hindsight, did encounter.

Now they're One ForAll and All For One

Princess Anne Civic Organizations Find That There's Strength In Unity

Journal and Guide (September 29, 1962)

Top photo. *Bottom left kneeling:* Jerry McCoy, Earl Smith, Robert Fentress, and Michael McCoy. *Second row, standing, left to right*: Angela McCoy, Carroll "Elaine" McCoy, and Denise McCoy. *Third row, standing, right to left*: Jerry Britton, Rubye McCoy, Jean McCoy, Ernestine Hodnett, and Unknown.

Second photo. *Left to right, kneeling*: Shelton Sheppard, Michael Melvin, Andrew Gills, and Thornton Russell. *Middle row, standing, left to right*: Sylvia Gilchrist, Marjean Russell, Gale Sanderson, and Patricia Jones. *Third row, standing*: Unknown, Carolyn Wilder, Theodore Wilder, Franklin Melvin, Vernice Sanderson, and Jerry Jones.

Third photo. *Left, kneeling*: Samuel Stephenson and Robin Towns. *Standing*: Mary Stephenson, Angela Smith Earl Stephenson, and Roxanne Stephenson.

The above photos are of those Negro children who were approved to transition by the state and whose parents intended for them to participate in the desegregation movement. Though there were initially. thirty-eight students approved, they all did not attend that first year.

Chapter 6

The Impact

The First Weeks of School

Note: some names have been changed to protect privacy.

There were only two Negro students attending Kempsville Elementary in 1962. Rubye Renà McCoy was in the fifth grade, and Carroll Elaine McCoy was in the second grade. This chapter will focus on the beginning of the mental and emotional turmoil from the second grader's perspective.

There was a total of twenty-five children in Mrs. Spence's class. Twenty-four were White, and then there was me, the lone *Negro*. During this first week, I was met with numerous life lessons (even though I didn't know it at the time). First was the bus ride. I'm sure the driver had been instructed to seat us in the front of the bus for observation purposes, but our parents had already instructed us to sit in the front if given the opportunity. As I remember it, Renà and I walked down the lane to the bus stop (unescorted by our parents) without conversation. I think she was as afraid as I was. As mentioned at the beginning of the book, I developed a nervous stomach, as referred to by our family physician, Dr. Kanacis.

Ma-Mè and Daddy had done everything that they knew how to prepare us for this event. We attended numerous hours in these secretive empowerment meetings to prepare us for what might occur. However, in my adult opinion, though I do understand the adults' intentions, I believe that some of the turmoil that occurred could have been resolved with kids just being kids.

I remember numerous scenarios were presented: "If this happens, do this." If we had been left to figure it out on our own, I believe, at my age, some of my anxiety would not have occurred, or perhaps it would have been less severe.

I was the child who was always being told to mind my business and go to another room because grown-ups were talking. So perhaps I heard more than I should have during that time. I remember going into my bedroom closet that backed up to my parents' room with a mason jar to my ear. (It was something I had learned from *Captain Kangaroo* and *Romper Room*, two children's shows that aired locally, or from *Highlights*, a Scholastic Reader that my mom received monthly for us. I'm not sure where it came from as sometimes, there were pages torn out or seek-and-find puzzles and other activities already completed. I believe that one of her White coworkers gave them to her after their children had finished with them.) Anyway, I could hear what my parents were talking about. Whenever they went into their bedroom and closed the door, I knew there was something worth hearing (with my nosy self).

For a year prior to the first day of school in 1962, when I was to transition to Kempsville Elementary School from Betty F. Williams Elementary School (the only all-Black school in Princess Ann County, Virginia, at the time for our region of the county), at least monthly, we were driven by my dad to meetings to discuss next steps in the integration process. As the new school year neared, those meetings became more frequent; I want to suggest every week, but that may have been my overactive mind. In hindsight, nothing could have prepared me for what was yet to come.

We were the only two at the bus stop that first year. Once we entered the bus (Bus 82, I still remember the bus number), there would be N-words slurred from side to side and spitballs thrown from the back to the front, where the bus driver could not determine who the culprit was. At Christmastime, we received a gift given by the White kids who rode the bus who said that they had taken up a collection for me and my sister—only to open it to find chicken and rabbit poop. We would find spit in our hair, and there was the tag game of passing our "cooties" from one person to the next. Then there was the name-calling chant using the N-word: "Eeny, meeny, miney, moe. Catch a [nigger] by the toe." And they referred to us as ugly, dumb, stupid, and so on.

Usually, the issues were always centered around me as I was never one to be belittled. And though I had been cautioned by our parents to ignore them, I found that difficult at six years old and would shoot off my mouth, exclaiming the same derogatory comments right back at them or saying, "Your mama!"

In direct contrast, Renà never received the same treatment as she was so sweet and mild-mannered and had learned the art of ignoring them. The only issue that she ever had was defending me. A lot of the "tar baby," "black as night," "nappyhead," and other comments related to the color of my skin or race were not directed at her as she was, in many cases, as fair-skinned as the White kids were, and my mom always hot-pressed our hair so that it was neat and well-groomed. At the end of most days, Renà returned home looking as neat and tidy as she had been sent to school. On the other hand, you could always count on me returning home looking as if I had been in a war zone—clothes disheveled and hair all over the place.

The bus driver of Bus 82, Mrs. Mitler (fictitious name), was always very apologetic for the White children's treatment toward us. She would say that she would inform the school principal of our mistreatment (and I believe that she did), but no consequences were given to my knowledge as the derogatory behavior continued.

The driver was always pleasant to us, and she would make sure during Halloween, Christmas, and Valentine's Day that we received the same snack that she provided the other kids on the bus (home-baked cookies, crafts, and a reindeer candy cane at Christmas and heart-shaped candy for Valentine's Day). I can honestly say that due to her kindness, we knew that we would be greeted by her in the morning with warmth and again in the evening, which was the last White face seen when we stepped off the bus. This encouraged me, in some small way, to try again the next day. I didn't share every incident with my parents as I somehow knew that this thing that we were doing was important.

Lasting Impressions

Sometimes words said can impact a young child for life.

During the first few months of school, I was also confronted with numerous classroom ordeals that had transitioned from the bus to the classroom.

In the classroom, there were twenty-five students: twenty-four Whites and me, the lone *Negro*. One day in September, my teacher announced to the class that she had observed some negative behavior during the week and needed to reassign desks. I was already in the front of the class in the teacher's eye view.

However, my teacher—let's call her Mrs. Spence (fictitious name)—employed a strategy of allowing her students to assist in making the rules of the class. After a week or so of school, on a Friday, the teacher had assessed her class as teachers do and determined that seating arrangements needed to be changed along with some new rules of classroom operation, as she saw a need to readjust her classroom management.

During this announcement to the class, she also commented to that class that she had five Carols in the class (me being one of them), and she needed a unique way to be able to distinguish between them when speaking. There was Carol Sampson, Carol Rodgers, Carol McSweeny, Carol Morgan, and me, Carroll McCoy. While soliciting input from the class and overlooking the snickers and muffled comments about the "nigger" Carol, the teacher decided to refer to us by our last initial. This meant that there would be a Carol S. and a Carol R. There were three *m*'s, two of which were *Mc*, so she decided that there would be a Carol M. and a Carol Mc (pronounced Mac). And by the time it came around to me, the class was in an uproar discussing if I would be referred to as the "Black" or "nigger" Carol. I'm not sure why she didn't capitalize on the fact that my name was spelled with two *r*'s and two *l*'s, but it seemed to me, in my six-year-old mind, that I was being made fun of. And of course, I didn't want to be referred to as the "Black" or "nigger" Carol. So I boldly raised my hand and announced that I wanted to be called by my middle name, "Elaine," as that was what I was referred to at home anyway.

That weekend, I shared what had happened on Friday with my oldest sister, Vera, who was livid. She immediately told my mother and father, who discussed the incident point by point with me so that they were clear on exactly what had happened.

They discussed calling the principal but determined that with all the other issues that I had encountered in the first week, it was probably better to set up a meeting to discuss *all* the concerns. Being called "Elaine" was the least of *my* worries as I was frequently referred to as "nigger," "coon," "spook," "blackie," "stinky," "ugly," "monkey," "nappyhead," and so on. I even had spit hocked in my face and, frequently, in the back of my hair.

I'm taken back to those days and remember that throughout my life, for years, even as an adult, when verbally referred to as Carroll (my God-given name), I would feel some kind of way, a bit irritated. My second oldest brother, Ronnie, would *always* call me by my first name as an irritant or dig. I think it was because he knew my unrealized distaste for the name. And of course, I would return the favor by calling him by his middle name, Alexander. I never took the time to really evaluate these feelings until I was an adult. *Carroll* was the name that my mother purposefully spelled as a male or as a last name with the double *r* and double *l*.

I can hear Ma-Mè saying, "When we gave you your name, we wanted you to get opportunities that other Black girls may not get just because of being female and Black."

The motivation for that name came from Dianne Carroll, who was the first Black female TV star in the late fifties to early sixties that represented more of the middle class that my parents were striving to maintain. And she said *Carroll* was the spelling of some White men's first name. She continued to say, "We thought that, on paper, no one could determine race or sex."

It wasn't until I entered my doctoral program for educational leadership much later in life that I was forced to begin to confront the issue of why I didn't use my first name through an emotional intelligence module that was required by one of my professors.

As an adult, until this time, I always signed my name *C. Elaine M. Smith*. I was well-known professionally locally and nationally in my field this way.

More recently, while drafting this book, I took significant time to delve into and process just why I felt this way about my first name. I know now that it was because of the derogatory comments and the way I was made to feel about my name being the "Black Carroll" so many years ago in the second grade. At that time, I was made to feel that being Black was a negative thing, even though I was taught at home that I should be "Black and proud." But when I went to school, I didn't feel that way.

At the age of six and seven, I just didn't have the maturity to rationalize that concept.

As an adult, after September 9, 2011, when it was required that all identification revealed the name on your birth certificate, only then did I begin to use my first name on paper. My friends and colleagues did not know who Carroll Smith was. I would say, until then, perhaps I didn't know who I was either. I believe that God set forth that situation to assist me to be able to examine the factors of my life to come to a better understanding of how I became the compassionate person that I am today. To understand not just who I am but whose I am. I am a child of God.

When you hear about the Civil Rights Movement in the South, Ku Klux Klan meetings are often referred to, but seldom do you hear about the "secret meetings" that Blacks had when planning a movement. I remember going a long way from home in the dark (it may not have been more than a few miles; however, it seemed a long way to my five/six-year-old self), then going in the back of a building (a church I think) and down some dark stairs to a room that seemed, to me, like a dungeon. (My teacher read to the entire class after recess the Cinderella story about a castle, a prince, and the dungeon where Cinderella was made to live. My mind may have conjured up this image). Needless to say, I had a vivid imagination.

Anyway, when we attended these meetings, we were surrounded by adults who discussed racial incidents in the community (a lot of which I didn't understand). I do remember, when the topic of schooling and buses was on the agenda, we were directed to pay close attention. We were told, "Don't let them [the White people] do this and that." By the end of the summer of 1962, I was a nervous wreck.

The months and weeks approaching the official opening day of school put me in what I know now as a state of anxiety that often manifested itself in my upset stomach. My parents missed the signs as, in my opinion, they were so involved in planning for the movement. No one considered the impact this would have on a child so young, but I believe my parents felt that because my sister and I would be together at the same school on the same bus, we would be able to handle the endeavor.

Typically, I was the child who always spoke my mind (I was in trouble a lot because of my mouth), was quite independent, and wasn't afraid to speak in front of adults. When it came to integration, nobody asked us how we felt about what was happening! As a child of that culture during those days, you did what you were told and asked no questions.

The cause was too important not to consider moving forward, and because we had not yet experienced racism, they must have felt that we were the best choice for our family.

Ma-Mè, What Are Cooties?

The dictionary defines *cootie* as a noun (plural *cooties*): "informal, (1) a louse, especially one affecting humans, as the body louse, head louse, or pubic louse; (2) a child's term for an imaginary germ or disease that one can catch by touching a person who is disliked or socially avoided."

Though there were numerous negative encounters that I experienced in the early years, the one that I viewed as the most annoying and daily thorn in my side was when some of the White children (mostly boys) would play the game "you've got her cooties" and touch me and pass it around to the next person like tag.

As if I had some disease. This game would be played all day every day. I had never heard anything like that other than to play tag, but I quickly realized that it was mean-spirited, and I found myself saying all day long (even on the bus), "Don't touch me!"

Then they figured out that I only needed to be touched once in order to pass the *cooties* around to each other all day or to start the game over someone else physically touching me again to reverse who the tagger was. For the first few months, this occurred frequently. But as the students got to know me, it subsided with my classmates but continued with those outside my class, mostly those who rode my bus, which sometimes included a couple from my class. Even if I was in line to go to the restroom or lunch, there was always a wide distance between me and the next person because they did not want to catch my cooties. I never understood why the teacher or other adults did not put a stop to the ridicule as they often witnessed the bullying but turned a blind eye to it. As the year progressed, Mrs. Spence (fictitious name), my teacher, would redirect students when she witnessed it.

Unfortunately, it often occurred when she was not present. Initially, I was told to tell her when it occurred, but it happened so frequently that I would be tattling all day. I learned to deal with it myself, which was not a wise choice as this often led to the situation becoming a shoving match. When I did tell, it did not stop the behavior.

In hindsight, I now realize that the career path that I chose as a special educator specializing in behavioral management and, more recently, developing programs for kids who exhibit antisocial behaviors (or what is now coined as bullying) and restorative justice has a direct relationship to my treatment in elementary school.

It is my opinion and has been proven that bullies have underlying unresolved issues that include poor self-esteem; therefore, they are projecting their feelings of inadequacy onto others. I wish I had a better understanding of that concept when I was younger.

Nevertheless, it is obvious why I advocate for social-emotional skills training in schools for all students, especially with the current worldwide COVID-19 pandemic and the anxiety and depression of children associated with it.

As a classroom teacher and with other supervisory positions held in education throughout my career, I have always advocated for positive behavioral supports in school for the victim of bullying and for the bully themselves (boys and girls).

After my parents had the meeting with the principal, I was informed by my parents and the teacher who announced in front of the class that I should tell an adult whenever it occurred.

I believed that she would inform their parents but could not understand why it continued to occur. I assumed that they would be chastised at home. I knew that if my parents instructed me to deter from behavior and I defied their direction, then I would experience an unpleasant encounter that I wanted no part of. It wasn't until much later that I understood that some of the students were simply modeling behaviors that they had witnessed from others and even at home. Maladaptive behavior is learned, but (in my opinion) it can be unlearned, and the home plays a vital role in correcting antisocial behavior.

Mind you, Princess Ann County (Virginia Beach, Virginia) was quite rural during those times, and in my area (not yet a community per se), there was a huge potato/pea (I think) field in front of our house where all the kids played when there were no crops planted.

I couldn't understand why some of the same children that I played hide-and-go-seek, racing games, made mud pies, made four-leaf clover bracelets and necklaces, caught lightning bugs (fireflies), and climbed trees with before integration started were the same ones who ostracized me in the company of their age-mates at school.

I even remember, as a child, going to the Blacks-only beach. Although I knew that we were not to cross over to the White side of the beach, the fun we had playing in the water and eating the fried chicken, homemade rolls, and potato salad lunches that Ma-Mè had made outweighed anything negative.

I eventually got it! The next few years would prove to be the beginning of my life's lessons in navigating adverse situations.

1962

October 1. James Meredith becomes the first Black student to enroll at the University of Mississippi. Violence and riots surrounding the incident cause President Kennedy to send five thousand federal troops.

1963

An estimated 62 percent of Americans—73 percent of Northerners and 31 percent of Southerners—believe Blacks and Whites should attend the same schools.

Two African American students, Vivian Malone and James A. Hood, successfully register at the University of Alabama despite George Wallace's "stand in the schoolhouse door"—but only after President Kennedy federalizes the Alabama National Guard.

For the first time, a small number of Black students in Alabama, Louisiana, and Mississippi attend public elementary and secondary schools with White students.

Fifty-six Black students—among a total student body of about thirty thousand—attend white beach schools. Princess Anne County and the city of Virginia Beach merge.

Most Oceanfront hotels, restaurants, and attractions drop Whites-only policies, and the beach sands open to Blacks.

My third-grade year at Kempsville Elementary may have been the most pivotal time of my life. The 1963 school year was a tough year. Not only had Renà changed schools due to her being promoted to the sixth grade (Kemps Landing Intermediate School), I found myself isolated due to there being no other children who looked like me at the school. The younger students, same age-mates, and the older children chastised me regularly. I was ostracized most of the time. On the bus to school, in the single-file lines into and around the building, in class, outside of class, in the lunchroom, at recess, in the bathroom, and on the bus on the way home.

That was the year that I began to learn to be comfortable with myself and by myself—visibly anyway. I knew how to put on a brave face and pretend that the ridicule did not bother me, though I often complained at home of an upset stomach (anxiety by today's standards).

This facade proved to be one of many skill sets that I obtained during this time, like striving to be the best at everything that I engaged in.

That year, most kids in the school had learned that I was a bit athletic. My family called it being a "tomboy," but I could do most physical activities well (run faster, jump higher, kick a ball harder, throw farther, etc.). I think it stemmed from growing up around farm land and having to do my share of chores around our home and my grandfather's farm. Most boys in my class—and one boy in particular (let's call him JC)—hated that I could beat him in almost everything, academically and physically. More details regarding JC will be presented as the story proceeds.

Opposition to Public School Integration in Princess Ann County, Virginia

Not only were there many Whites who did not want segregation to end and some who supported integration in various ways, but there were also African Americans who did not want change. One distinct incident stands out in my mind.

I was in the third grade, now the *only* African American student in Kempsville Elementary as my sister Renà had graduated from the fifth grade and had been promoted to the sixth grade at Kemps Landing Intermediate School. On this day, I had been permitted to be excused to the restroom. When I entered the restroom, there was no one else inside. I did what I needed to do, and as I washed my hands, a familiar woman from the custodial staff who we'll refer to as Ms. Vicky the maid (fictitious name) entered the restroom.

She began to empty the trash and wipe down the sinks. As I threw my paper towel into the trash can, she approached me, backing me into a corner (perceived through my seven-year-old eyes) with an angry tone. "Who do you think you are? You and your family are no better than the rest of us! I know who you are. I know your daddy and your mama,

Ruffin and Rosana. And things were just fine before all this mess began. It's hard enough getting them to accept us [the African American staff] around here. You don't belong here! I wish y'all had left things alone!"

I was terrified! I stood there with what I imagined was a dumbfounded look on my face but said nothing. I was taught to respect adults. With tears in my eyes, I left the restroom and returned to the classroom but said nothing to my teacher. The rest of that afternoon, I could think of nothing else but why Ms. Vicky was so angry at me! All I had done was thrown my trash into the trash can. Maybe I should have put it in the bag that she carried in her cart.

Of course, when I got home from school, I shared my day with my mother. She immediately called the school to set up a meeting.

When I asked why that lady had treated me that way, my mother explained that there were some people who looked like us that were satisfied with not having the same educational opportunities as White people or having to pay (poll taxes) in order to vote (which often was a hardship for Black people who did not have good jobs like White people with benefits). She felt what we were doing may jeopardize her job.

She said that it was "ignorant thinking," and as long as Blacks continue to think like that, our race would never progress. I didn't understand all of what she was saying, but I did get that what Ms. Vicky had done was wrong and that she would handle it.

Ma-Mè was at the principal's office when he entered the building the next morning. He asked me what had happened. I told him and was written a pass to class. I'm not sure what the outcome of the meeting was. I know she was called to the office, but Ms. Vicky never said another word to me.

Chapter 7

Informal Suspension

May was coming soon, and we all were practicing for the Presidential Fitness Award ceremony, where we would show off our athletic ability to the whole school by grade level. The fifty-yard dash and shuttle run were events that I usually won, but JC had tied me and beat me (not by much) in the challenge a couple of times and was always teased that the "N-word" girl beat him. I knew it had to be a clear win to beat him so it would not be a close call as I felt in one of the previous cases where he won—my head and foot were over the line, but he was given the win.

On the day of the event, we were directed that when we completed our activity, we could play in the area where the monkey bars were. There were swings, see-saw, and monkey bars, and there were group activities in which we could participate.

As anticipated, I beat JC in both events, and he was furious. The other kids whispered and mocked him as we were presented with the first- and second-place ribbons. I went directly to the area where we had been directed to after the event. I was often ostracized, so it wasn't unusual that I found myself on the swings alone.

I noticed that several boys were crowded around JC, being loud and laughing. JC then approached me from behind and swung me backward off the swing, and my head hit the sand. He then slapped me hard enough to turn my cheek. I knew that the term "turn the other cheek" that my mom and dad so often referred to could not be this, so I responded. I was able to wrap my legs around him and flip him on his back, and I began to punch him in the face to the point of making his nose bleed. It was then that the adults intervened. I believe that they waited because JC not only bullied me but other students as well, and he needed a good kick in the pants.

We were both sent to the principal's office. We were called in separately. He went first and was allowed to go back to class, but I had to spend the rest of the day in the office. (It probably was not a very long time as the physical fitness event was ending when we left the event.)

Technology was limited during those days. As mentioned before, we only had a home phone (which was a party line), a radio, a black-and-white TV, and a record player. Both of my parents worked and were not readily available to speak on the phones in the offices at their places of work unless it was an emergency. My mom was called at work. During this time, my mom was a nurse's assistant at Holmes Convalescent Home, and my dad drove a supply truck at the Norfolk naval base.

I was given a sealed envelope for my parents and told that I could not return to school until they could accompany me. I later was informed there was a letter stating that my parents needed to come to the school on Monday morning.

That ride home on the bus usually took forever, even though we only lived 1.2 miles from the school, and I was the first stop. That first year, we were the last picked up in the morning and the first to be dropped off in the evening (I assume to alleviate behavioral issues), but that day, in antic-ipation of what would occur when I got home, the bus ride home seemed quicker than usual. When my feet landed on the ground and I gazed down the lane, I immediately got a sickening feeling in my stomach. It had been determined the year before that I had developed what was explained to me as a nervous stomach. I often experienced dry heaves (scared to death of what would happen).

As I slowly walked toward the house, I could see my daddy's work truck in front. I pushed that letter deeper into my pocket as I knew I was going to get it! Renà, who got home first, met me at the bus stop at the end of our lane, trying to be as encouraging as she could. But she feared what would happen next as well as we had been told to avoid con-frontation at all costs, and my mom had already informed her that the school had called.

When we got closer to the house, we could see Daddy sitting on the front porch. I thought, *If he doesn't already know, I'll wait until after church on Sunday to give them the letter.*

With each step, the emotions swelled to the point that I was crying uncontrollably by the time we got to the house. My mother had already gotten the call from the principal and notified my dad. He greeted us both, told Renà to go in the house, and asked me to take a seat on the steps. He took one look at my tattered clothes and messy hair and said, "Hard day?"

"Yes, sir," I said.

"What happened?" he asked in a calm voice.

"After we raced and I won, this boy—who is the same one who is always passing my cooties around to everybody on the playground—was mad because I won the race, pulled me off the swing, slapped me, and spit in my hair. I swung him by his shirt until he fell, and I punched him back as hard as I could. His nose started to bleed, and the teacher broke us up."

While I was explaining, I noticed a small brown paper bag in the left pocket of his jacket. I recognized the shape of what was inside as I could see the white sticks sticking out where the bag was twisted tight. It was candy! Tootsie Roll Pops, to be exact. In our home, living in a rural area on farmland, it was a rare treat to receive candy. And surely, I wouldn't be getting any after the day that I'd had at school.

Daddy continued to talk, but he noticed that I was distracted by what was in his pocket. To my amazement, he pulled out two candies. One was grape, and one was cherry. He asked, "Which one do you want?"

"Red," I exclaimed. (Red has always been my favorite color).

I took the candy quickly but was hesitant to unwrap it or put it in my mouth. He unwrapped his and put it in his mouth and encouraged me to do the same. As we continued to talk, he reminded me of topics covered during our "secret" meetings and lessons learned from the Bible and stressed the importance of being proud of who I was.

At one point during the conversation, he pulled out his Tootsie Roll Pop and commented that he could almost see the chocolate middle of the lollipop. He asked me to check mine, but I was not as far along as he was.

We continued to talk about my experiences at school. He asked what I wanted to be when I grew up, what kind of house and car I wanted, if I wanted to get married, have children, and so on. He asked if I could see the middle of my candy yet, and as I pulled my candy from my mouth, the middle was revealed.

At that very moment, he said, "Look at yours, and look at mine."

I did.

He said, "People are like these Tootsie Roll Pops. We are all different on the outside but exactly the same on the inside." He continued, "It takes all flavors of people to make up this world, good and bad. *No matter what you look like on the outside, we're all the same on the inside.* Whether you're black, white, red, orange, or yellow, there is good and bad in every race. No one is better than you, and you are no better than anyone else."

I told my dad that all the White kids at school said that I was dumb, stupid, Black, nappy-headed, poor, and ugly. I couldn't understand why the same kids that played with me at home said these things, made fun of, teased, and laughed at me at school with the other kids. Why?

"It makes me scared to go to school," I said. "And next year, Renà won't be there again, and I'll be all by myself."

My dad replied, "Those kids just don't know any better. We are simply different. But you listen to me. I know it's hard, but what you and Renà are doing is important, not just for our family but for all the future Negro children so that they can have the best books and opportunities just like the White children do. I bet more children will attend next year."

He continued, "Do you remember the story that Ma-Mè told y'all about that little Negro girl in her state of Louisiana who was the first to go to school with White children? She did the same thing that you're doing."

He said that he wondered if she had similar talks with her parents, who wanted to make things better for her and other Negro children. "Because of her, you now have the opportunity to do the same."

He further stated, "Don't you let nobody tell you that you can't be what you want to be or do what you want to do. Hard work and determination will take you far. Times are changing, and I may not live to see the changes that are coming, but you'll be able to look back on these days and remember that I told you so."

I shared how scared I was some days to even go to school because of being made fun of and being made to feel that something was wrong with me and my family like we were dirty, stupid, or had some disease.

"I always have to fight the boys." The ugly things that I heard made me feel that I had to prove them wrong. I wasn't dumb or ugly.

My dad stopped me in midsentence. "Coconut [a term of endearment that only he called me], hold your head up high and remember, you are smart, pretty, a McCoy, and most of all, a child of God. That means something!

"Everything happens for a reason, and I may not be able to explain in a way that you can understand why you're treated the way you are, but whenever you feel that fear is taking over, pray and ask God to show you the way. Do you hear me?"

"Yes, sir," I replied.

"Just say, 'Lord, help me.' He hears you. And in each situation, say, 'Thank you, Lord.'"

I have to chuckle as I write this because those who know me know that I'm heard frequently saying "thank you, Lord" for no apparent reason to others even today as an adult.

I can still hear the conviction in his voice: "It takes all flavors of people. We're *all* the same on the inside, no matter what color you are. If you work hard and treat others as you want to be treated, God will take care if you."

He began to hum and sing a hymn that his gospel group performed. It was "God Will Take Care of You" by Mahalia Jackson. "Be not dismayed whatever betide, God will take care of you. Beneath his wings of love abide. God will take care of you. God will take care of you. Through every day along the way, he will take care of you. God will take care of you."

My dad was the tenor with a male quartet and sang around Tidewater with a group called the Martineers, I think. I researched but could not come up with a definitive answer as to what the group's name was as there are very few people still alive who remember. I was told by other family members that he sang with a couple of groups, one of which was named Only Four, and that the name changed a few times. I remember, as a little girl, it was my daddy and three of my uncles (Uncle Leonard, Uncle Igenter, and Uncle Wilton). And as time went on, some of them left and others joined. (Today, I wonder if the name was indicative of it being only four of the six McCoy brothers.)

As Daddy sang, he rushed me to finish my candy as Ma-Mè would not be too happy that we ate candy before dinner, and it was getting to be that time.

We were never taught to belittle others. We were taught to do unto others as you would have them unto you. This had been one of the family discussions that we had on Sunday mornings, among other things. It just dawned on me that perhaps those discussions were a strategic plan on my parents' part in preparation for the movement. Amazing!

By the end of that year, though it had been quite difficult to have been the only Black child in the school that year, I looked forward to more children from the community who looked like me joining the effort as other Black parents became more comfortable with the idea of public school integration. The next year, more Negro children did come!

April 16. Martin Luther King Jr. is arrested and jailed during anti-segregation protests in Birmingham, Alabama.

He writes his seminal "Letter from Birmingham Jail," arguing that individuals have the moral duty to disobey unjust laws.

May. During civil rights protests in Birmingham, Alabama, Commissioner of Public Safety Eugene "Bull" Connor uses fire hoses and police dogs on Black demonstrators.

These images of brutality, which are televised and published widely, are instrumental in gaining sympathy for the Civil Rights Movement around the world.

June 12. (Jackson, Mississippi) Mississippi's NAACP field secretary, thirty-seven-year-old Medgar Evers, is murdered outside his home. Byron De La Beckwith is tried twice in 1964, both trials resulting in hung juries. Thirty years later, he is convicted of murdering Evers.

August 28. (Washington, DC) About two hundred thousand people join the March on Washington. Congregating at the Lincoln Memorial, participants listen as Martin Luther King Jr. delivers his famous "I Have a Dream" speech.

Chapter 8

Purpose-Driven Life

At that time, my dad had limited education, but the profound analogy that he used could not have been clearer: "People are like Tootsie Roll Pops." It was at that moment, as a seven-year-old, when I realized that this whole integration struggle thing was bigger than us. We were opening doors for others so that they, too, could be given the opportunities that were afforded to people who did not look   like us. I was doing what needed to be done for a better life for myself, other children, my children, and my children's children. And so it was.

1963

South Carolina's Clemson College became the first integrated public school in that state. Gov. George C. Wallace of Alabama stood in a doorway at the University of Alabama in a symbolic attempt to block two Black students from enrolling in 1963. The attempt failed.

In the North, attempts were also made to combat segregation. After a suit brought by Black parents in 1960, the school system of New Rochelle, New York, was, in 1961, ordered by a federal judge to be desegregated.

Similar suits followed in other cities.

Public transportation and accommodations. The fight over education overshadowed efforts to achieve integration in other areas, but moves against segregation in public transportation did gain wide notice.

September 15. (Birmingham, Alabama) Four young girls (Denise McNair, Cynthia Wesley, Carole Robertson, and Addie Mae Collins) attending Sunday school are killed when a bomb explodes at the Sixteenth Street Baptist Church, a popular location for civil rights meetings. This also led to the deaths of two more Black youths.

The Merger—When a County Becomes a City

The Town of Virginia Beach was organized in 1906. In 1952, after the population growth of World War II, the town became an independent city separate from Princess Anne County. The existence of Princess Anne County ended in 1963 when it merged with the city of Virginia Beach.

1964

Bayside High opens in the fall as an "integrated" school with four Black students. Citywide, 127 Black students attend White schools.

January 23. The Twenty-Fourth Amendment abolishes the poll tax, which originally had been instituted in eleven Southern states after Reconstruction to make it difficult for poor Blacks to vote.

Summer. The Council of Federated Organizations (COFO), a network of civil rights groups that includes CORE and SNCC, launches a massive effort to register Black voters during what becomes known as the Freedom Summer. It also sends delegates to the Democratic National Convention to protest—and attempt to unseat—the official all-White Mississippi contingent.

July 2. President Johnson signs the Civil Rights Act of 1964. The most sweeping civil rights legislation since Reconstruction, the Civil Rights Act prohibits discrimination of all kinds based on race, color, religion, or national origin. The law also provides the federal government with the power to enforce desegregation.

The Civil Rights Act of 1964 is adopted. Title IV authorizes the federal government to file school desegregation cases. Title VI prohibits discrimination in programs and activities, including schools receiving federal financial assistance.

The Reverend Bruce Klunder is killed protesting the construction of a new segregated school in Cleveland, Ohio.

August 4. (Neshoba Country, Mississippi) The bodies of three civil-rights workers (two Whites, one Black) are found in an earthen dam six weeks into a federal investigation backed by President Johnson. James E. Chaney (21), Andrew Goodman (21), and Michael Schwerner (24) had been working to register Black voters in Mississippi and, on June 21, had gone to investigate the burning of a Black church. They were arrested by the police on speeding charges, incarcerated for several hours, and then released after dark into the hands of the Ku Klux Klan, who murdered them.

Voting Rights. To circumvent the Fifteenth Amendment to the US Constitution, which guaranteed voting rights to Black men, the 1901–1902 Virginia Constitutional Convention required voters to prove their understanding of the state constitution and imposed an NAACP poll tax of $1.50 to be paid annually by registered voters.

New voters had to pay $4.50, a large sum of money in those days. The Democratic majority in the General Assembly appointed all election registrars. As intended, these measures reduced voting by poor Whites and Republicans, and within ninety days, more than 125,000 of the 147,000 Black voters in the state had been stricken from the rolls.

Literacy tests—such as Virginia's requiring a "reasonable explanation" of any part of the state constitution—disappeared when the Civil Rights Act of 1964 stipulated that anyone with a sixth-grade education was presumed literate. The Twenty-Fourth Amendment, ratified in 1964, outlawed poll taxes in federal elections. In 1966, the US Supreme Court banned it in all elections. Events such as "Bloody Sunday" in Selma, Alabama, persuaded President Lyndon Johnson to propose a Voting Rights Act, which he signed into law on August 1965.

1965

Virginia Beach begins to allow parents to choose Black or White schools. The number of transfers increases.

February 21. (Harlem, New York) Malcolm X, a Black nationalist and founder of the Organization of Afro-American Unity, is shot to death. It is believed the assailants are members of the Black Muslim faith, which Malcolm had recently abandoned in favor of Orthodox Islam.

March 7. (Selma, Alabama) Blacks begin a march to Montgomery in support of voting rights but are stopped at the Pettus Bridge by a police blockade. Fifty marchers are hospitalized after police use tear gas, whips, and clubs against them. The incident is dubbed "Bloody Sunday" by the media. The march is considered the catalyst for pushing through the Voting Rights Act five months later.

August 10. Congress passes the Voting Rights Act of 1965, making it easier for Southern Blacks to register to vote. Literacy tests, poll taxes, and other such requirements that were used to restrict Black voting are made illegal.

August 11–17. (Watts, California) Race riots erupt in a Black section of Los Angeles.

September 24. Asserting that civil rights laws alone are not enough to remedy discrimination. President Johnson issues Executive Order 11246, which enforces affirmative action for the first time. It requires government contractors to "take affirmative action" toward prospective minority employees in all aspects of hiring and employment.

STOP Incorporated

Established in 1965, STOP's purpose was to provide a range of strategies and initiatives that have quantifiable and potentially major impacts on the root causes of economic disadvantages. STOP focused its efforts on areas impeding the achievement of self-sufficiency among hardworking low-income wage earners.

Several initiatives identified for service delivery include child care, crisis intervention, education, employment, health, housing, nutrition, and youth services. This organization helped numerous Blacks from my community, and as you will read in a later chapter, it helped me too. It is the youth services program that provided me the opportunity later in life to recognize that there were other employment opportunities outside of working in the fields.

1966

October. Oakland, California— the militant Black Panthers are founded by Huey Newton and Bobby Seale.

In 1966, the Presidential Physical Fitness Award was finally created by President Lyndon B. Johnson after conducting the second national fitness survey in 1964–1965.

May Day. In the early sixties, May Day was a holiday that many Americans celebrated, but relatively few can explain why. Depending on your age, and perhaps your culture, you might associate May 1 with a festive occasion with documented physical fitness activities (much like a school carnival) like dancing around and braiding a maypole with long multiple-colored ribbons or watching military tanks proceed through Moscow's Red Square on a black-and-white television on the evening news. For me, it was the maypole.

Dressing in my Sunday clothes (my mom or oldest sister always tried to match my dress with the ribbon that I would be using in braiding the pole) and getting my hair hot-combed straight with Royal Crown or Bergamot hair grease, it was a special time. Many parents and other adults attended (White people) from the county, and it was stressed to all students that the expectation was to be on our best behavior.

Presidential Fitness Award

The President's Council on Youth Fitness, in the hopes of making American kids fit enough to compete with the Swiss (who were outranking the American kids by far), initiated a pilot study of a national fitness test—the Presidential Fitness Challenge. It had its issues and was seen in schools more like a military exercise for kids to get fit as opposed to being a fun fitness program aimed at improving the health of American kids.

By 1966, President Lyndon B. Johnson created the Presidential Physical Fitness Award, the name of which was later changed to President's Challenge Youth Physical Fitness Awards Program. In 1983, the United States Congress declared May as National Physical Fitness and Sports Month. The Presidential Physical Fitness Test is comprised of six activities: curl-ups, pull-ups, push-ups, the sit and reach, the thirty-foot "shuttle run," and the one-mile endurance run.

I was a country girl and was used to running, jumping, and chores that required strength. I was always trying to outdo the boys whenever I could, so when it was time to compete, I was intrigued by the possibility of winning awards for what seemed to just be fun to me.

1967

B. F. Williams Elementary school in Virginia Beach, Virginia, converts to a plan that assigns students to an attendance zone by residence, not race. The school becomes majority White. Three Black schools remain. The Virginia Beach Human Relations Council charges that there has been "no effort to make Negro schools so attractive that Whites will prefer to attend them instead of their current choices."

April 19. Stokely Carmichael, a leader of the Student Nonviolent Coordinating Committee (SNCC), coins the phrase "Black power" in a speech in Seattle. He defines it as an assertion of Black pride and "the coming together of Black people to fight for their liberation by any means necessary." The term's radicalism alarms many, who believe the Civil Rights Movement's effectiveness and moral authority crucially depend on nonviolent civil disobedience.

June 12. In *Loving v. Virginia*, the Supreme Court rules that prohibiting interracial marriage is unconstitutional. Sixteen states that still banned interracial marriage at the time are forced to revise their laws.

July. Major race riots take place in Newark (July 12–16) and Detroit (July 23–30).

1968

The Supreme Court orders the states to dismantle segregated school systems "root and branch." The Court identifies five factors—facilities, staff, faculty, extracurricular activities, and transportation—to be used to gauge a school system's compliance with the mandate of *Brown* (*Green v. County School Board of New Kent County*).

In a private note to Justice Brennan, Justice Warren writes, "When this opinion is handed down, the traffic light will have changed from Brown to Green."

Amen! "The Voting Rights Act authorized federal supervision of voter registration wherever fewer than half of eligible voters were registered, which included virtually all of the South.

These efforts, supplemented by Black freedom schools, registration drives, and voter rallies, tripled the number of Black voters by 1968, and the number continued to grow thereafter.

—Virginia Historical Society

1969

Virginia Beach, Virginia, schools fully integrate. Students are assigned to schools by geographic boundaries. Segregated Union Kempsville High School closes to become an alternative school. About 36,500 students attend Beach schools. About one in ten are Black. Seaboard Elementary is renamed Princess Anne Elementary and becomes mostly White. Seatack Elementary stays almost entirely Black.

Suffolk, Virginia, converts its all-Black high school to a junior high and integrates.

The Supreme Court declares the "all deliberate speed" standard is no longer constitutionally permissible and orders the immediate desegregation of Mississippi schools (*Alexander v. Holmes County Board of Education*).

1970

By the 1970s, according to studies by Gary Orfield, the South had become the nation's most integrated region. In 1976, 45.1 percent of the South's African American students were attending majority White schools, compared with just 27.5 percent in the Northeast and 29.7 percent in the Midwest. These gains occurred in the context of the second great controversy of the school desegregation effort—busing.

The controversy came to a head in the Supreme Court's 1971 decision, *Swann v. Charlotte-Mecklenburg Board of Education*, one of the first attempts to implement a large-scale urban desegregation plan. Swann called for district-wide desegregation and allowed for the use of busing to achieve integration, finding that the times and distances involved in the desegregation plan were no more onerous than those involved in the busing already undertaken by Charlotte for non-desegregation purposes. Court-ordered busing, as it came to be known, was fiercely attacked, not least by the administration of President Richard Nixon. Busing was criticized as undermining the sanctity of neighborhood schools, as social engineering, as impractical and unworkable, and as intrusive and inappropriate judicial meddling.

Busing drew a great deal of public attention. Critics largely overlooked the facts that few students were bused for the purpose of desegregation and, indeed, that busing worked—especially in the South, where school districts are often countywide and include both central cities and suburbs.

April 4. (Memphis, Tennessee) Martin Luther King Jr., at age thirty-nine, is shot as he stands on the balcony outside his hotel room. Escaped convict and committed racist James Earl Ray is convicted of the crime.

April 11. President Johnson signs the Civil Rights Act of 1968, prohibiting discrimination in the sale, rental, and financing of housing.

1971

April 20. The Supreme Court, in Swann v. Charlotte-Mecklenburg Board of Education, upholds busing as a legitimate means for achieving integration of public schools.

Although largely unwelcome (and sometimes violently opposed) in local school districts, court-ordered busing plans in cities such as Charlotte, Boston, and Denver continue until the late 1990s.

The federal government orders Virginia Beach to bus students to Seatack Elementary because geographical boundaries are not sufficient to create a diverse school.

Norfolk, Virginia, implements crosstown busing to fully integrate its schools.

The last Black high school in Chesapeake, Virginia, "Crestwood" becomes a junior high. Black high school students are dispersed among the White high schools.

1972

Plans to turn I. C. Norcom High School in Portsmouth, Virginia, into a technical school to attract Whites meet with student protest.

I earned my high school diploma (the first of four degrees to follow) at age sixteen from Kempsville High School. My plan was to attend college since my father had passed away. I, as his offspring, was able to financially use his GI Bill to further my education.

I decided to major in education after having an employment opportunity to work with disabled adults at what was then called TARC (Tidewater Association for Retarded Citizens) and had a rewarding experience. During that time, I had very little involvement with the guidance department, but when college became my goal, I set up an appointment with my counselor. To make a long story short, she discouraged me to go to college as she said, "You will never be selected to teach school."

(Not saying why, but I knew exactly what she meant.) She only said that the education field was difficult to get into, and my response was "so was this school!"

She went on to encourage me to become a beautician and complimented my hairstyle, saying, "Wouldn't that be a more appropriate profession?"

I thanked her for her time and left, but I did not give up on my dream.

God's Plan!

This same year, legislation was introduced by Congress after several "landmark court cases establishing in law the right to education to all handicapped children." Thus, a new segment of education began: special education.

Also in 1972, President Nixon—partly in fear of Alabama governor George Wallace's independent presidential campaign—mounted an attack on busing and asked Congress to ban it. Although President Nixon's effort failed, the drive for desegregation slowed. In 1974, the Supreme

Court, in *Milliken v. Bradley*, a case involving the Detroit metropolitan area, effectively halted busing at a city's borders. The Court's 5–4 decision blocked a city-suburb desegregation plan in Detroit that would have involved busing across school district boundaries. Ignoring evidence of state governments' past and continuing involvement in housing and school segregation, the Court said that "local control" was an important tradition in education. The decision allowed for proof of "interdistrict violations" while placing heavy burdens on plaintiffs in future cases.

This prompted most universities to begin programming for the disabled in the education departments. On November 19, 1975, Congress enacted Public Law 94-142, also known as the Education for All Handicapped Children Act of 1975. Not only did I have experience working with the disabled from my summer employment, but I realized from that experience that if the adults that I had experienced that summer had early intervention when they were much younger, perhaps they would have had more of an opportunity to reach their highest potential and live a productive life. Through my studies, I found that some students were deemed to need special education due to inappropriate behavior students exhibited in school.

As I furthered my studies and looked closer at societal and environmental factors that impact children, I reflected on my own experiences. And thus began my quest to study human behavior and the many factors that promote social-emotional growth in children. God allowed everything in my life to happen, even the negative events that impacted me in a way that would prove beneficial. "What the devil meant for evil, God meant for my good" (Genesis 50:20).

Throughout my career, continuing challenges for equal educational opportunities included, but were not limited to, witnessing disproportionate assignment of minority students to special education programs while White students were disproportionately assigned to gifted and talented programs. Disparities in the rates and severity of discipline imposed on minorities as compared to White students were also concerning. Also of concern was the use of tests for making high-stakes decisions about students' educational opportunities when such tests adversely affect minority students and are not shown to be required by educational necessity.

With continuing migration, especially from Spanish-speaking and Asian countries, the issue of equal educational opportunity for non-English-speaking students remains increasingly central. A good public-school education should be afforded to all students regardless of one's zip code.

1973

Section 504 of the Rehabilitation Act is passed, prohibiting schools from discriminating against students with mental or physical impairments.

The Supreme Court rules that states cannot provide textbooks to racially segregated private schools to avoid integration mandates (*Norwood v. Harrison*).

The Supreme Court finds that the Denver school board intentionally segregated Mexican American and Black students from White students (*Keyes v. Denver School District No. 1*). The Court distinguishes between State-mandated segregation (de jure) and segregation that is the result of private choices (de facto). The latter form of segregation, the Court rules, is not unconstitutional. The Supreme Court rules that education is not a "fundamental right" and that the Constitution does not require equal education expenditures within a state (*San Antonio Independent School District v. Rodriguez*). The ruling has the effect of locking minority and poor children who live in low-income areas into inferior schools.

Early on, in my family, we were never taught that there was a difference between people. I'm sure my older siblings had a better understanding of the racial tensions that were apparent during those days, but Renà and I had not developed a mindset of division. I believe it was for this reason, my parents chose us to be a part of the end to desegregation in public schools.

Throughout my early life, I often wondered why Vera, George Jr., and Ronnie (my oldest siblings) were not also made to go to the White schools. It was not until I began this cathartic process of writing this book that I came to have a better understanding of my parents' infinite wisdom. I believe they knew that the older children were more likely to have greater and more severe difficulty in high school, as was witnessed through the stories televised on our one black-and-white TV and the firsthand accounts of incarcerations, killings, and harassment by police told to them of what was happening locally and in other states. I believe they felt that violent attacks and altercations would be less likely to occur in young children.

As a parent myself, reflecting on the turmoil and chaos that were evident during those years, I can only imagine what it must have taken for them to make the final decision to put their then-feisty six-year-old (me) and their very quiet mild-mannered ten-year-old (Renà) in the forefront of the movement. I'm sure it was not an easy decision, but at some point, you must take a stand.

They did.

Reflections

As I reflect on my life, each milestone, each open and closed door, each opportunity I believe was preordained by God, that I would be one of the ones chosen for such a time of unrest. My sister Renà's experience was different from mine as she was mild-mannered, very fair-skinned, and rarely experienced opposition. Myself of a darker hue and mouth almighty, I encountered verbal and physical adversity on a daily basis. The issues that Renà encountered were only because she was defending me. But as quiet as it's kept, I really didn't need her help and was always able to handle my business—socially, emotionally, and physically.

I now know that God positioned me at the right time, in the right family, and purposefully in the right place, choosing me for *all* the adversity that I would encounter throughout my life. And it was he who ordered my steps with *favor*.

I toyed with several titles for this book and found myself asking, "How can I best explain in a title what this book is about?" As I pondered, I reviewed how the PCL/PAC had to maneuver the progressive goal of public-school integration in a substandard roundabout way. They made the commitment not to accept the authority's ignoring their request and the repeated negative responses of no or "wait a little longer" when the law clearly said differently; they communicated with others (Norfolk 17 leaders) who had previous knowledge of the process and what obstacles to avoid making the same mistakes. They studied the law; they disseminated information face to face and/or at social gatherings in secret and sometimes publicly made bold movements to force the hand of authority so their request for transferring schools would less likely be denied.

Acknowledging the way in which the PCL/PAC was forced to strategically, but within the law, take the back road around the public-school administrator's purview who were reluctant to move forward with integration policy for public schools in Princess Anne County and giving homage to the actual (as referred to by the New Light community) back road where I lived and where it all began for my family—Whitehurst Landing Road, it is the author's opinion that *Back Road to Progress* could not be a more fitting title for this book.

Chapter 9

Hidden Figures

I have been a hidden figure in the shadow of my truth for many years, but I would venture to say my story is not unique. Some may say unique because of the age of the child who encountered such traumatic experiences, but I am not the first and certainly not the only one. There are numerous undocumented stories of African American civil rights struggles and the numerous generational stories of how individuals and families (as in my case) were committed to overcoming the struggles of segregation. People who just wanted a better life for themselves and their children.

As a culture, many of my ancestors—slaves and beyond—survived through storytelling. It was the way information was disseminated. However, through the years, we have lost the art of storytelling. As we became more educated, we were expected to read about history and learn about history in schools—never mind that what was in print only represented a one-sided view. Many facts have been purposefully left out. Telling our truths to, at a minimum, the youth in our families who today have little compassion for the struggle for equality that their forefathers encountered will strengthen us as a culture. Those who stood up to injustice and those who supported in the background are equally as important to the progression of justice and equal rights in our country.

Unfortunately, today, these stories are usually heard by our youth only after their loved one or a familiar person passes away. It is at those moments that they wished they knew more, but the authentic expression of truth has died with the deceased. I encourage the readers to document their story (regardless of their ethnicity) and share it so that not only the younger generation in your family and your culture but the overall human community has a better perspective of your truth.

America is the melting pot of the world, and with a more precise understanding of these historical challenges and triumphs, we become a stronger nation. Let no one else tell your story. If you're like me, your past can and does impact the future. I'm stronger because I had to be. I'm smarter because I've made mistakes and learned from them. I'm happier because of the sadness that I've encountered but with a clearer understanding of why things occurred as they did. And now I'm wiser because of my understanding of my purpose and God's favor in my life.

No matter how good or bad my life has been or is, I wake up each morning thankful that I still have a life. I am mentally stable (some may disagree) and physically healthy and strong. I work for causes, not for applauses. I live life to express, not to impress. I don't strive to make my presence noticed, but I strive to make my absence felt.

In light of the current dynamics of the racial climate in our nation today as evidenced by the horrific incident that occurred a few years ago in 2017 in Charlottesville, Virginia, where racial tension was the foundation of chaos, the reason a life was lost, and for those acts of injustice that have occurred before and since, it is my hope that this literary work (from a six-year-old child's perspective), in a small way, depicts how blatant racial bigotry can have a lifelong impact on children (both negative and positive). Those children grow up to be adults.

What many people fail to realize is that what happened in Charlottesville, Virginia, was not a new phenomenon. Racial tension has periodically reared its ugly head since the 1800s, though it has not been widely broadcasted. With the technological advances of today, when something happens, we all know the second after it occurs. The racial divide continues on many fronts in our nation today, and it's up to each individual to confront it in our own way when it occurs.

Educational Racism

In hindsight, I now realize that the career path that I chose as a special educator specializing in behavioral management and, more recently, developing programs for kids who exhibit antisocial behaviors (or what is now coined as bullying) and restorative justice has a direct relationship to my treatment in elementary school.

It is my opinion and has been proven that bullies have underlying unresolved issues that include poor self-esteem; therefore, they are projecting their feelings of inadequacy onto others. I wish I had a better understanding of that concept when I was younger.

I believe that my passion for advocating for those less fortunate, particularly children, and taking an active stand against injustices in our society is a direct reflection of my own life experiences. I know what it feels like to be ostracized for being different. I know what it's like to have an ongoing feeling of low self-esteem, having to always be two steps ahead in order that my worth is recognized while others are rewarded as they revel in mediocrity. Therefore, it has become my life's work to improve the educational experiences of all children. More specifically, those who have special needs, with a laser view on the enhancement of what they *can* do—not what they *can't* do. In other words, focusing on their ability, not their disability. Every student who struggles in school is not eligible for special education.

Some students struggle because they learn differently. They may need more time, or perhaps education has not been a positive factor in their parents' lives and, therefore, is not a priority in the home. It has been my experience in the thirty-plus years of my career that what these students require, in many cases, is someone who can build a relationship with them in the school setting, providing relevant instruction that takes into consideration the whole child, not just the curriculum.

High expectations, accountability, consistency, and a loving heart can go a long way with students, especially those who are simply unmotivated with potential behavioral concerns, as they, too, can work to their fullest potential and be positive contributors to society.

Discrimination comes in so many forms and should have no place in schools. Regardless of a student's zip code, race, ethnicity, religious belief, or disability, every child has the right and should be given the opportunity to excel to his fullest potential.

Teachers are in strategic positions of influence to support and encourage love and dismiss hatred in schools. I believe that social skills, character development, and life skills (or whatever is the current term used to teach children how to respect differences) should be regularly taught in schools, not just in special education.

Every student can benefit from a skill set of engaging in inclusivity. I have digressed a little from the main topic, but in my opinion, it is aligned with the topic of discrimination.

Pros and Cons of Segregation

We are a culture of proud people, and some believe that during segregation, we were better off because we had to be self-sustaining communities, relying on each other for our basic daily needs. We had farmers who grew organically grown food before it was popular, tailors, seamstresses, carpenters, banks and bankers, grocery stores, convenience stores, liquor producers, doctors, nurses, electricians, transportation services, teachers, plumbers, and so forth. Then there are others who argue that integration was the best thing that could have occurred.

I have mixed feelings due to my life experiences and upbringing. I believe both are true. Integration did benefit many and allowed some to have opportunities that they otherwise would not have had, even though the way was paved through their suffering and experiences due to racism. The reason that I vacillate regarding integration's beneficial qualities is that my dad also was of the mindset that if we are to survive as a community, we must support each other and keep our monies within the community. That was one of his main reasons for securing his plumbing license after the military and encouraging others to become skilled blue-collar professionals also. In our nation, as we struggle with the current economic crisis and the state of our educational system, we could take a lesson from that today. His role as the advisor of the PCL/PAC was to recruit persons interested in working for the same just cause.

As for education, during the days of "separate but equal," this concept was a misnomer. We were indeed separate but certainly not equal. I believe that the genuine comradery, diligence and dedication to education that the black teachers had then, accepting the mammoth responsibility for each negro child to succeed, refusing to allow us to fail academically, socially or emotionally, promoting the concept of economic equality is what dissipated with the integration of public schools. Yes, there were a few white teachers who showed compassion and were sound teachers but the ongoing pride to be change agents to promote educational equality by the few black teachers positioned in the white schools was lost or at least diminished because they too were attempting to survive in their professional careers.

The teachers (who were also neighbors) had experienced a level of racism throughout their own history and vowed to prepare us to stand strong in the face of adversity and to always pursue endeavors with integrity. These were my dad's words regarding public school integration: "If it's good enough for their children, it's good enough for mine!"

As mentioned earlier, before college, I only had two Black teachers—Mrs. Rosalyn Freeman in the first grade and Mrs. Jean Siler, tenth-grade typing. Both were strong females who each reinforced valuable character development in me. Though my natural demeanor has always been to be outspoken (not always in the most positive way), I believe my first-grade teacher, who was a friend of the family, groomed me for what I would encounter the next year during integration. We were in the first brand-new all-Black elementary school and often had administrators from the county and/or state department visiting our school. Each grade level had representatives who acted as tour guides and were interviewed by these visiting adults. I was always chosen.

Mrs. Freeman taught me leadership skills, such as volunteering to assist when there was a task to be done, speaking in complete sentences, giving eye contact, and being sure to use my manners. Never be afraid to speak up but always think before answering. Mrs. Siler taught me to take pride in my appearance, speech, and actions. In her tenth-grade typing class, we were graded on our appearance and speech as, once a week, we were required to dress for success and participate in mock employment interviews. She taught me about carrying myself as a young lady, not following the crowd, making decisions for myself, and not being influenced by what was popular. Other than my parents, she was the only other adult with whom I discussed my wish of wanting to become a teacher. I shared that my guidance counselor had discouraged me from becoming a teacher, saying "that could never be" and to become a beautician, which was an honorable profession. Without speaking against the counselor, she told me that times were changing, and just like she had, I, too, could become an educator.

We can dismantle all the artifacts that celebrate or represent racism in America, *but* until the hearts are changed at the very core of those in America who believe that there is no place in our country for anyone who does not look like them or think like them, and policy reflects those changes, the need for facilitating racial cohesiveness will continue.

My life experiences, educational research, and spiritual guidance have brought me to a place of peace and understanding. I'm convinced that this story, ultimately, is *"his story."* It is history because its contents are facts that led up to the beginning of the end of the segregation of public schools in Virginia Beach, Virginia.

It is *"his story"* because I believe that God allows all things (good and not so good) to happen for a reason. Through God's grace and mercy, he anointed and guided me through every step of my life's challenges, and there have been many.

Though both my parents (George Ruffin McCoy and Rosana Holloman McCoy) are deceased, I thank God for their insight to propel me and my sister Rubye, who passed in 2014, into the forefront of this local historical event.

Courageous Conversations

As a country, we must acknowledge that there have been hundreds of years of racial discourse, and some progress has been made. We have recently begun to dismantle artifacts, such as Robert E. Lee statues that celebrate or represent some of the darkest days of American history. However, considering the current dynamics of the racial climate in our nation, it is the author's hope that this small peek into the past, from a child's perspective, will encourage courageous conversations throughout our country.

These conversations should begin at home when children are young and impressionable. As parents, it is our responsibility to teach our children what is right and wrong. Left undone, the world becomes their teacher. Today, with the impact of television, movies, and social media, a lack of morals is often at the forefront of what sells.

As parents, we should be the greatest influence in our children's lives. I can still hear my father's profound words as we enjoyed our Tootsie Roll Pops on the porch the day I got into trouble for fighting at school in the third grade. He said, "Baby, it takes all flavors of people to make up this world. Just like these Tootsie Roll Pops [I had cherry, and he had grape], we may be different on the outside, but we're all the same on the inside. No matter if you're red, purple, black, or white, ain't nobody better than you because of the color of their skin. If you work hard and keep God in your life, you can be whatever you want to be. Do you hear me!"

I smile as I reminisce. He later expounded on his flavor analogy when we talked about me making the boy's nose bleed. He said, "What color was his blood?"

I responded, "Red."

He then said in a very matter-of-fact way, "And what color is your blood when you bleed?"

Again, I said, "Red."

And he said, "You see. We're *all* the same!"

I never forgot his analogies and have used them on many occasions when working with children who have been bullied.

Chapter 10

Lessons Learned

As I conclude, I want to thank God for choosing me for a time such as then. Thank you for the resilience, fortitude, and perseverance needed to withstand such treatment. To all those bullies, the cootie passers, the nigger callers, and those who spat on me, knocked books from my hands, pulled my hair in the reading circle, pushed chairs away from mine so that they would not sit close to me (as if I had a disease), and those who stood by and watched and laughed—I forgive you. I know you were then a product of your environment. You were taught hatred or had to be a part of the actions of the majority or you, too, would have been ostracized. My hope is that you've learned to judge people by their character, not by the color of their skin, and treat them accordingly. And today, in your adult life, you are willing to stand up for what is just even when it is not the most popular thing to do.

To Mrs. Spence, my third-grade teacher, I now know that perhaps you were under extreme pressure from parents, other teachers, the community, and administrators. Though you were always nice to me, through my seven-year-old lens, you ignored much of what could have been eliminated. Whether it was purposeful or because you were overwhelmed with the responsibility of the situation, I understand. As an educator, and knowing how the system works, I'm sure you were chosen for that situation; and like me, you were trained (or not) to use your own life experiences to respond as you did. To avoid conflict at all costs—and that you did well by ignoring.

To that one little White girl in elementary school, NR (you know who you are), who befriended me. Perhaps it was because you, too, were being bullied, or perhaps it was because you genuinely cared and were taught fairness, kindness, and compassion. But whatever the case may be, thank you for being the friend that I needed to get through that tough year. I often wondered if you told the story of our connection to your family and friends. I am thankful for the experience.

Each challenge, throughout my life, assisted in molding me into the person that I am today, good or bad.

"When people show you who they are, believe it!"

Today, my acceptance of *all* people is a direct reflection of how I was impacted by my dad's words. "There is good and bad in every race. It takes all flavors of people to make up this world, the good and bad."

I'm stronger because I had to be. I'm smarter because I've made mistakes and learned from them. And I'm happier because I've known sadness and realized God is the author and finisher of my life. I'm now wiser because I understand that history can repeat itself, and I'm able to reflect and see that some progress has been made. However, there continues to be much more work required in order for communities, our nation, and the world to be healed.

No matter how good or bad my life is, I wake up each morning being thankful that I still have one and that, hopefully, those that I have encountered in my life are impacted in a positive way.

I now work for causes, not for applauses. I live life to express, not to impress. I don't strive to make my presence noticed. I just strive to make my absence felt, all the while, giving God all the glory for my life, such as it has been and is.

I have been a hidden figure until now, but I would venture to say my story is not unique. There are others in all cultures who have stories to share so that we all have a better understanding and appreciation for the contributions made that have molded our nation (good or bad).

I encourage others to document their story and share it so that generations (X, Y, and Z and so on) in your families, within and outside of your overall culture, will have a more precise understanding of the challenges as told by someone who lived it in order to heal the racial tensions that currently plague the world—but more importantly, the issues that divide these United States.

Let no one else tell your story. Tell it while it still can be told from a first-person narrative. Do not let it be tainted by someone else's perception of what it was like or told as in our history books, leaving out details that spin a different narrative.

I say this because in 2009, I read an article in our local newspaper referencing the 1962 desegregation movement. It stated that the events took place "without a hitch." That comment is a direct reflection of who the narrator was.

I believe history can and does impact lives (some good, some not so good). Again, I'm convinced that, ultimately, my life's story is *"his story"* (God's story), as he has ordered my actions every step of the way, molding me into the person that I am today: Dr. C. Elaine McCoy Smith, a real McCoy.

Appendix

Virginia Public School Integration Time Line at a Glance

Virginia's public school system was segregated from its very beginning in 1870. Courts ruled that separate facilities for Blacks and Whites were legal as long as they were equal.

Segregated schools were rarely equal. Black students had poor buildings, textbooks, and facilities compared to White students. White teachers were paid, on average, three times as much as Black teachers in 1915. NAACP lawyers began filing suits in federal court in the late 1930s for equal teacher pay and schools. Lawsuits helped to improve all levels of schools for African Americans, but education remained unequal.

In 1951, African American students led by sixteen-year-old Barbara Johns walked out of Robert Russa Moton High School in Farmville to protest the school's poor condition. Students and NAACP attorneys Oliver Hill and Spotswood Robinson filed a lawsuit in federal court to demand integration instead of equal schools. Their case became part of the landmark case *Brown v. Board of Education of Topeka, Kansas*. The US Supreme Court ruled in 1954 that "separate but equal" in public education is unconstitutional.

Virginia senator Harry F. Byrd called for "massive resistance" to the *Brown* decision. Virginia's legislature passed laws to prevent desegregation. Many school districts resisted by closing schools for periods ranging from a day to five years. In some districts, all White students left the public schools rather than attend integrated schools.

By 1968, the US Supreme Court was dissatisfied with Virginia's slow compliance with federal desegregation guidelines. The court ruled that districts must "ensure racial balance in schools."

Local school boards changed school boundaries, built new schools, and used busing to create integrated schools. Every school district in Virginia experienced some level of change from segregated to integrated schools.

Lawsuits against busing began to chip away at this success, and the resegregation of schools began. By 1988, integration peaked in the US. Afterward, schools in many cities became more segregated, not less.

Despite some setbacks, school desegregation and diversity remain a top priority for the US Department of Education. In 2006, the US Supreme Court declared that school integration remains a "compelling national interest." The struggle for school desegregation is an important part of the American quest for justice and equality. The goal for the future is to ensure equal educational opportunities for everyone throughout the Commonwealth of Virginia.

Unfortunately, we are still in an era when one's zip code often determines the quality of education that is received in public education. Today, for the past two years, the impact of the COVID-19 and the need to find an alternative way to educate our children virtually has stifled the progress of our children even more. The 2023 *Report on Condition of Education* released by the National Center for Education Statistics (NCES), the statistical center within the US Department of Education's Institute of Education Sciences (IES), presents the challenges of the COVID-19 pandemic in every dimension of American education, from prekindergarten (preK) and elementary school through college and beyond.

NCES Commissioner Peggy G. Carr stated, "These challenges include declines in math and reading scores during the pandemic and greater numbers of students seeking mental health services.

Separate and unequal policies did not begin in the fifties and sixties. For the reader who is interested to research more detailed information regarding historical civil rights events in the state of Virginia, this simplified chronology is provided.

Civil Rights at a Glance

1831—Blacks barred from schools.

1870—Segregated public school system was created.

1896—*Plessy v. Ferguson*. Supreme Court rules racial segregation legal—"separate but equal" doctrine.

1924—Racial Integrity Act passed. Native Americans are barred from White schools.

1936—Dovell Act is passed. Gives scholarships for Black college students to be educated out of state.

1940—Federal court rules Norfolk School Board violated Fourteenth Amendment by not paying Black and White teachers equally.

1948—President Truman orders the desegregation of armed forces. Chesterfield, King George, and Gloucester Counties ordered to equalize Black and White schools.

1950—Gregory Swanson enrolls in UVA Law School. First African American student at White school in Virginia. Black students were admitted to Virginia Tech and the College of William & Mary for programs not available at Virginia State College in the next five years.

Virginia leads the way to Brown v. Board of Education

1951—Students in Farmville protest unequal conditions, then sue for an integrated school. The lawsuit becomes part of *Brown v. Board of Education*.

1954—Supreme Court in *Brown v. Board of Education of Topeka, Kansas*, rules "separate educational facilities are inherently unequal." The base school at Fort Myer is integrated by the Department of Defense. Catholic schools in Richmond Diocese enroll sixty Blacks in formerly White schools.

1955—*Brown II*. Supreme Court rules that school desegregation must take place with "all deliberate speed."

Virginia massively resists

1954—The Defenders of State Sovereignty formed to oppose the *Brown* decision. African American students sue for admission to White public schools.

1956—Senator Byrd encourages "massive resistance" to school desegregation. Massive resistance laws are passed to "prevent a single Negro child from entering any White school."

1958—Federal courts order nine White schools in Warren County, Charlottesville, and Norfolk to admit Black students. Governor J. Lindsay Almond closes those schools.

1959—White parents win the suit against school closings in Norfolk. Federal and state courts rule massive resistance laws unconstitutional. Closed schools are reopened with limited integration. Arlington admits Black students to White junior high schools.

1959—Prince Edward County, refusing to integrate, closes public schools, locked until 1964. White students attend private schools. Tuition grants for "segregation academies" begin.

1959—Virginia approves the Freedom of Choice plan. Few Black students apply to transfer to White schools. Fewer are accepted.

1962—Public school segregation ends in Princess Anne County, Virginia

1963—Surry School converted to a White-only private school. County's Black schools remain open. Few White students attend public school for the next ten years.

1964—Supreme Court orders Prince Edward County schools reopened.

1964—Civil Rights Act passed.

1964—Public schools are opened to Native Americans.

1968—All public colleges now admit both Black and White students. Private colleges follow. Supreme Court ends "freedom of choice" plans.

1969—Court ends state tuition grants to children attending segregation academies. Grants cost taxpayers $20 million.

1970—Governor Holton enrolls his children into previously all-Black schools in Richmond. Busing for racial balance begins.

1974—Supreme Court limits busing in Richmond.

1986—Norfolk becomes the first city in the country to end busing for racial balance.

1988—Desegregation of US public schools generally peaks. After this, schools in many cities become more segregated.

References

"American civil rights movement." https://www.britannica.com/event/American-civil-rights-movement.

Autherine Lucy and the University of Alabama. http://www.americaslibrary.gov/aa/marshallthrgd/aa_marshall-thrgd_lucy_1.html.

Civil Rights Training Modules. https://blogs.extension.wisc.edu/civilrightstraining/civilrights101/.

"Desegregation of Virginia Education (DOVE): Timeline." www.odu.edu/library/special-collection/dove/timeline.

"How Dolls Helped Win Brown v. Board of Education." https://www.history.com/news/brown-v-board-of-education-doll-experiment.

Infoplease. "Civil Rights Timeline." https://www.infoplease.com/history/us/civil-rights-timeline.

Infoplease. "Parks, Rosa Louise." http://www.infoplease.com/encyclopedia/people/social-science/reformers/parks-rosa-louise.

"NAACP." https://www.history.com/topics/civil-rights-movement/naacp.

Potter, Halley, and Kimberly Quick. "The Secret to School Integration." https://www.nytimes.com/2016/02/23/opinion/the-secret-to-school-integration.html.

Princess Anne County Training School. http://www.museumsvb.org/room/union-kempsville-museum.

"Red Summer of 1919: How Black WWI Vets Fought Back Against Racist Mobs." https://www.history.com/news/red-summer-1919-riots-chicago-dc-great-migration.

"Rosewood Massacre." https://www.history.com/topics/early-20th-century-us/rosewood-massacre.

Smith, Tom. 1992. "Changing Labels from 'Colored' to 'Negro' to 'Black' to 'African American.' *Public Opinion Quarterly*, volume 56, issue 4 (Winter): 496–514. https://doi.org/10.1086/269339.

"Southern Christian Leadership Conference." https://www.britannica.com/topic/Southern-Christian-Leadership-Conference.

"The Civil Rights Act of 1964: A Long Struggle for Freedom." https://www.loc.gov/exhibits/civil-rights-act/civil-rights-era-timeline.html.

The Journal and Guide. http://thenewjournalandguide.com/.

The Leadership Conference Education Fund. https://civilrights.org/edfund/.

The Leadership Conference on Civil and Human Rights. https://civilrights.org.

The Leadership Conference on Civil and Human Rights 2016 Legislative Priorities (Senate). https://civilrights.org/resource/the-leadership-conference-on-civil-and-human-rights-2016-legislative-priorities-senate/.

The Norfolk 17: A Personal Narrative on Desegregation in Norfolk, Virginia, in 1958 1962. https://www.amazon.com/Norfolk-17-Personal-Narrative-Desegregation/dp/0805973052.

"Tulsa's 'Black Wall Street' Flourished as a Self-Contained Hub in Early 1900s." https://www.history.com/news/black-wall-street-tulsa-race-massacre.

About the Author

The face of adversity is quite familiar to Dr. C. Elaine McCoy Smith. In 1962, as a second grader, she was one of two students to first integrate Kempsville Elementary School in the city of Virginia Beach in Virginia, then known as Princess Ann County.

Beginning at the age of five, her parents supported her on a journey of learning experiences that were both negative and positive but all vital to her development. Those experiences propelled her into being the passionate and compassionate person that she is today.

Dr. Smith, an educator, made it her personal and professional commitment to seek what is fair and just regardless of the political, social, or handicapping conditions of those who are less fortunate. She has spent her career in many roles in education and is currently an educational consultant and advocate, giving volume to muted voices often discounted due to various irrelevant issues, including race, gender, zip code, and/or disability.

She is best known locally and nationally as an expert in providing positive behavior interventions and supports (PBIS) to students in public and private schools, both academically and behaviorally. She is the founder and CEO of Coastal Virginia Special Education Advocacy, where she consults and trains local private/public agencies and parent groups. She is a wife, mother, and grandmother.

She is a member of Delta Sigma Theta Sorority Inc., Daughters of Isis, the National Association for the Advancement of Colored People (NAACP), and the National Council for Negro Women (NCNW)—all of which are public service organizations in which services are provided to women, children, and families in need of support. She is spiritually guided under the leadership of Bishop K. W. Brown and Elder Valerie Brown of Mount Lebanon Global Fellowship of Churches in Chesapeake, Virginia.